Sara Earns Her Ears

Sara Earns Her Ears

My Secret Walt Disney World Cast Member Diary

EARNING YOUR EARS: VOLUME THREE

Sara Lopes

Theme Park Press

Editor: Bob McLain
Layout: Artisanal Text

ISBN 978-1-941500-27-9
Printed in the United States of America

Theme Park Press | www.ThemeParkPress.com
Address queries to bob@themeparkpress.com

Contents

CHAPTER ONE

The Wonderful World of Color

"Why do you want to work for Disney?"

This was the most important question of my life. My answer would determine whether I would participate in the Disney College Program. It could make my dream come true.

I took a deep breath and started to think back to the day I decided I wanted to work for Disney. I was on a surprise trip to Disneyland for the first time on my own. My best friend, Holly, was visiting the parks for the first time, and I was honored to be her tour guide. I've always been a huge fan of Disney, especially the theme parks. Watching Holly experience the magic for the first time is something I will never forget.

Every night at our hotel we would hear music blasting from California Adventure, with colorful lights shooting into the sky near Mickey's Fun Wheel. We had no idea what was happening, so the very last day of our trip we decided to go see what was causing all of the commotion. We soon discovered that the music was coming from Disney's brand new water spectacular, World of Color.

After fighting through impatient tourists and cranky children, we managed to find a spot near the front right side of the viewing area. Little did we know how much magic Disney had in store for us that night.

The lights dimmed as we waited with anticipation. Music began playing, and beautiful fountains of light and color started dancing across the bay. Reds, greens, blues, pinks, and every color you can imagine shot and twirled toward the sky. As soon as the introduction faded and Ariel appeared on a screen of water, I was in awe. I had never seen anything as amazing and beautiful as what I was seeing at that moment. My heart raced along with the *Pirates of the Caribbean* theme song. Lasers, lights, and fire exploded on the bay in synch with the music. I had never been in so entranced by a show in my entire life. At the very end, when Jon McLaughlin's "So Close" began to play, tears started to form in my eyes. My entire childhood had just projected in front of me, and I realized just how big of a part Disney has been in my life.

From that moment, I knew I needed to be part of the Walt Disney Company. I needed to be part of the magic and learn how to create it for other people.

As soon as I arrived back home, I raced to my room to research possible Disney career opportunities on my laptop. After many Google searches, I came across a website called The Disney College Program. Its description was a single, eloquent sentence: "When the time of your life is life-changing."

I soon discovered that the Disney College Program is an internship for college students in both Disneyland and Walt Disney World. Those accepted into the program would have the opportunity to live, learn, and work in one of several roles offered at both of these resorts.

Like most children, I grew up with Disney. I watched *The Lion King* and *Aladdin* more times than I could count, and going to Disneyland made me the happiest girl alive. I was very shy when I was little, and the thought of going to a Disney park was one of the few things that would coax me out of my shell. In 8th grade, I worked on a year-long project that included a report and presentation all about Walt Disney. I learned so much about his life and what he experienced to accomplish his dreams that he became one of my biggest role models and inspirations.

When I was a freshman in high school, I got to travel to Walt Disney World for the very first time. I was blown away by its size in comparison to Disneyland. The fact that you had to take a bus or monorail to go to each park was such a strange concept! I was used to simply walking from Disneyland to California Adventure in a matter of seconds; traveling from Magic Kingdom to Epcot on a bus or monorail was such a strange concept. Unfortunately, we only had three days to explore all four parks before going on our Disney cruise.

I never would have guessed that the next time I'd visit Walt Disney World would be five years later as a cast member.

CHAPTER TWO

Preparing for the Application

As soon as I decided to apply to the Disney College Program, I began researching the various elements of the application, the different roles available, the classes offered, and the apartment options. College Program blogs and videos were my new obsession. I wanted to absorb all of the advice from previous cast members like a sponge. If someone on YouTube mentioned a tip about the application process, I scribbled it in my journal. I wrote a list of the top roles I was interested in, and explanations for each position. I created a list of pros and cons for each apartment complex, and even started to consider which park I wanted to work in during the internship. It consumed my dreams, both day and night, for an entire year before I was even able to apply.

There are two options for the Disney College Program location: Walt Disney World in Florida and the Disneyland Resort in California. You're allowed to choose one or the other, with the second as a backup, if you wish. Since I had experienced Disney World only once in my life, I decided to apply only for the internship option in Orlando. That program also accepts a much larger percent of individuals in comparison to Disneyland, giving me a better shot at getting in. Disney World also offered a specific marketing seminar not available in the Anaheim program, but I'll explain more about that later.

Applicants have three different options for program lengths. You can choose between working in the spring (January to May) or the fall (August to December). Both spring and fall have "advantage" options, which let you stay and work over the summer in addition to the original five months. There is also a quarter program, for students who attend colleges that do not run on the semester system. I chose the regular spring semester, since I was about to transfer schools a few months after returning from my program.

Various roles are offered as jobs during the internship, and you can indicate your level of interest (if any) for each when you apply. In the end, I decided that merchandise, attractions, and hotel concierge were my top three choices. Merchandise includes gift shops in the parks, as well as shops in Downtown Disney and in the resorts. Attractions means working at either a ride or show in one of the parks, and hotel concierge is part of the front desk cast members in the resorts. My "low interest" role choices were housekeeping, quick service food and beverage, custodial, and transportation. I put at least some interest in every single job offered during the program. I was willing to take any role they'd give me.

I decided on these top three role choices after a thorough investigation on blogs, websites, and YouTube videos. One blog that helped me understand the lifestyle of a college program participant, and actually inspired me to write my own blog about my program, is DCP Dreams Come True. It contains extremely detailed posts about moving to Florida, training, living situations, and what it's like to live in Walt Disney World. A cast member named Ashley, who participated in the Fall Advantage program in 2012 in quick service food and beverage, wrote all of the posts. During her program, she wrote about what it was like to work in outdoor food carts in the Magic Kingdom as well as at Epcot's Food and Wine Festival. Even though food and beverage was one of my low interest roles, Ashley's detailed descriptions made me even more excited to apply and participate in the program.

I already had a blog called The Disney Den, where I would post fun and interesting facts about Disney. When I decided to include the DCP as part of my blog, I added a site on Tumblr to use as an extension. Tumblr allowed me to connect with other potential participants who wanted to apply to the DCP at the same time as I did; it was nice talking to other people with the same dream. It also made me nervous. With the DCP rapidly growing in popularity, I realized that competition for its limited spots would be even fiercer than I had anticipated.

YouTube was very handy for learning about the DCP. There are endless video blogs with past and present cast members explaining their experiences and telling their stories. Disney even has their own YouTube channel dedicated to the DCP, including role description videos and advice from past participants about what it's like to move away from home, money management, and packing. Kelsie Doing Disney was the most helpful channel that I stumbled upon. She was a PhotoPass Photographer in Magic Kingdom and always uploaded helpful video advice about small details that many other YouTubers seemed to skim over. She had useful suggestions about how to ace the phone interview, what it was like to get up extremely early for check-in, homesickness, and how she enjoyed her days off from work. These kinds of videos also inspired me to start my own video blog of my experience during the college program, which I decided not to start until after I had applied.

As I was searching through Tumblr and YouTube, I noticed many past participants talked about the Disney College Program Facebook group. I decided to take matters into my own hands and search "Disney College Program Spring 2013" online. Sure enough, there was a group made just for applicants like myself! I requested to be added into the group, and as soon as I was accepted I religiously scrolled through the posts and statuses to see the kind of people I might meet during the program. It was amazing to see so many other Disney fans aiming for the same goal.

A few months before Disney opened the applications process, my friend Sara decided that she wanted to participate in the program as well. I was ecstatic! I was a little worried about the moving away from home all the way across the country for the first time by myself, but if Sara was accepted with me, we would be able to share this amazing journey together. I added her to the Facebook group page, and we quickly began making new friends before the applications opened up to the public. We even started to keep an eye out for potential roommates. Doesn't hurt to start early, right?

After a few weeks of getting to know people in the Facebook group, there were rumors swirling about when the applications would finally drop. Disney never announces the actual opening date, but instead gives an estimated time frame for each application period. In the previous year, the applications opened during Labor Day weekend in September, so we were all anxious to see if the same would happen for the Spring 2013 applications. Finally, word got out that an official date had been chosen. On Thursday, September 6, the applications would open for everyone.

I couldn't wait.

CHAPTER THREE

The Application

My alarm went off at seven in the morning, and my stomach immediately fluttered with anticipation. I jumped out of bed and hopped in my desk chair, nearly flinging my laptop open out of excitement. I hurriedly clicked on the web browser, typed in the DCP website, and smiled. There it was: the open application.

Today is the day, I thought. *Today is the day I apply to the Disney College Program.*

I didn't have time to apply right then, since I had class that morning. I was fidgety throughout calculus and couldn't focus on economics. I would constantly look at the clock and count down the minutes until each class was over. As soon as my professor finished explaining weather patterns in physical geography, I bolted out the door, to the parking lot, and into my car to drive to Sara's house. The internet connection in my house was unreliable and would drop at random moments, so we decided to apply together at her place.

When I arrived at Sara's house, I said hello to her mom and made a beeline to Sara's room. She had already submitted the first part of her application, but was still waiting for the email to invite her to the second portion. I plopped on her bed and opened the application, ready to finally start applying to the DCP.

The first part of the application asked for basic information, such as my name, which college I attend, my major, and my previous job experience. The next step required me to choose the Disney resort where I wanted to work and whether spring or spring advantage. I decided to only apply for spring in Walt Disney World, since I needed to come back over the summer and I've been to Disneyland multiple times. Florida was calling my name; I needed to return!

After I chose which term and which resort, I needed to rank each job role with my level of interest. As I previously mentioned, my "high interest" roles were merchandise, attractions, and hotel concierge, while my "low interest" roles were housekeeping, transportation, and quick service food and beverage. I didn't put any roles as "no interest" because I wanted every window of opportunity open to increase my chance of getting accepted into the program.

Ranking roles was the last part of the basic application. With great anticipation, I clicked submit and I was finished! The next part was the hardest: waiting. Applying on the day the application opens is definitely a huge waiting game. Since the website was bombarded with applicants at the same time, the system was slow to register everyone and send confirmation emails. Sara and I ended up waiting about an hour and a half for our confirmation emails, which were quickly followed with invitations to participate in the next section: the web-based interview.

The web-based interview was basically a personality test. It asked me questions such as whether I'm an outgoing person, whether I'm generally happy, whether I prefer to work alone or in groups, and whether I enjoy a fast- or slow-paced work environment. You had less than a minute to answer each question on a scale of "strongly agree" to "strongly disagree". I was nervous, since succeeding on this portion of the application would advance me to the phone interview, the most important component. If I didn't give Disney the "right" answers, I'd be thanked for my time and sent on my way. The online interview took me around 40 minutes, and as soon as I was finished, I was immediately invited for a phone interview.

A majority of applicants pass the web-based interview, but I do know some people who did not.. My advice is to answer with strong opinions. Most of the people who were not invited to the phone interview answered many of the online questions with "neutral". If you're neutral about many aspects of your personality, how is Disney going to know if you're a qualified candidate for the job? Keep in mind the type of people Disney would like to have work for them (confident, energetic, professional individuals), but also answer truthfully about yourself and your personality. If you don't pass the web interview, you can always try again during the next application period. Some people don't get accepted until their second or even third try.

We received the invitation to schedule our phone interview ten minutes after completing the web-based interview. After battling with a frustratingly over-populated website, I scheduled mine for the following Monday at 6:15 pm, while Sara's was the day after at 2:00 pm.

It was the longest four days of my life.

CHAPTER FOUR

Phone Interview

The days in between the application and my phone interview seemed to go by as slow as the line for Space Mountain during the holidays. More and more applicants were posting in the Facebook group about how their interviews went, what questions they were asked, and the duration of the interviews. Every night I studied a list of sample questions I found online and practiced my answers both in my head and out loud. I asked my parents for their opinion about some of my answers, and I brainstormed questions to ask my interviewer.

I woke up Monday morning with knots in my stomach. This was the day I would seal my fate. There was no possible way I could concentrate on the two classes I had that day, which were thankfully over by noon. The only problem left was trying to occupy my time and my mind while waiting for 6:15 pm to roll around.

The five-hour waiting process consisted of listening to Disney music, attempting to distract myself on the internet, studying my sample questions, talking to my mom, and playing the piano. The piano helped occupy my hands, since otherwise I was a nervous wreck. Around the 30-minute mark, I locked myself in my room and began pacing back and forth, constantly staring at my phone. I tried to release some of my nervous energy through writing in my journal, but ten minutes before the phone was supposed to ring I stopped and committed myself to solely pacing beside my desk.

I looked at the clock: 6:09.

More pacing.

Looked again: 6:11.

I couldn't handle it; the moment I've been anticipating for over a year is going to arrive in a matter of minutes.

Suddenly, the phone rang.

I looked down and saw a blocked caller ID, which meant only one thing: Disney.

I took a deep breath and answered the phone. A woman named Christine introduced herself and asked me about my day. She also asked about my first year in college, since I was a second year when I applied. After kind of breaking the ice, she began, "Why do you want to work for Disney?"

I had rehearsed this answer to the point of perfection by the time of my interview, and each subsequent question she asked me was one that I had either read in my study guide or heard about from someone in the Facebook group. She asked about my work preferences (indoor/outdoor, fast/slow pace), whether I had experience with cash, whether I'd spoken in front of a large group before, and whether I've lived with roommates. I felt confident about everything she was throwing at me, until she asked, "If you were a merchandise cast member, how would you make someone's experience magical?"

I froze. This wasn't anywhere in my notes. I wasn't sure exactly what to say, because in my head I thought it all depends on the situation, so I couldn't get myself to respond with anything specific. I slowly replied, "I would go out of my way to make sure the guests received above and beyond customer service and exceed all of their expectations."

I breathed a sigh of relief when we moved on to the next question, which was how I would handle an emergency. The rest of the interview went smoothly, and Christine reminded me that since I put some level of interest for every single role, I could have a chance at *any* of those roles. I acknowledged the possibility and answered her questions about the Disney Look. She asked if I had any tattoos that would be visible outside of a one-piece bathing suit, any piercings, or unnaturally dyed hair. After this, Christine asked if I had any questions, which was my cue to ask the questions I had thought of while I was practicing over the previous few days.

I asked her about the various languages I might encounter if I participated in the program, as well as recommended classes that could help with my degree as a marketing major. She told me that all different languages from around the world come to the parks, so it's hard to pinpoint some specifically, and she recommended the Exploring Marketing seminar I was planning on taking, as well as a couple other courses they offer during the program.

After she answered my questions, the interview came to a close. Christine explained to me that she has zero control over the acceptance process. All of her notes just get transferred to the group that is in charge of choosing who will be accepted into the program. I told her I understood, thanked her for everything, said goodbye, hung up the phone, and took a deep breath.

"YES!!"

I spun around and opened my bedroom door. My mom was beaming. Apparently she had listened to my entire interview and exclaimed that I had done a wonderful job. I was a little embarrassed, but more than anything I was relieved. I had finished the most important part of my application.

Now all I could do was wait. Again.

CHAPTER FIVE

The Waiting Game

My mind was at ease for the next couple of weeks, but I was still anxious to hear back from Disney as soon as possible. I rooted Sara on through text messages right before she had her phone interview the next day. She didn't feel as confident after her interview as I had felt after mine, but I knew she blew it out of the water.

We posted a joint roommate survey on the Facebook group to start keeping an eye out for people to potentially room with during the program. (See the appendix for a copy of the survey.) As a result of the survey, we met some of our closest friends, even though we ended up not rooming together. Katie and Giselle were the first two that we really hit it off with. We bonded over Harry Potter and favorite Disney movies. Like myself and Sara, Katie and Giselle had been best friends for years. Meriem and Emily were two other girls we connected with rather quickly through the roommate surveys, also through our mutual love for Harry Potter and Disney. These four girls were the first true friends I made through the Facebook group, so they were naturally our first choices for roommates if we all got accepted.

However, this was the problem. Everyone was so excited to post roommate surveys, meet other people, and make new friends that we all kind of forgot a huge detail: we weren't entirely sure we were all actually *doing* the program yet. Any day one of us could get an email from Disney with a heartbreaking sentence, "Thank you for applying, but unfortunately your application is no longer in consideration." This haunted us.

During the agonizing waiting period, I uploaded a video blog discussing my phone interview process. This also opened new doors to meeting new people who wanted to do the program, and it was my first step toward helping others learn more about the DCP and what they need to do when they apply. I absolutely loved helping people learn more about the college program, even though I was still learning much about it myself. I also began making friends with fellow applicants on Tumblr. This is how I met Christine.

Christine and I started talking through our Disney blogs. We were both so incredibly excited to potentially participate in the program and anxious to hear back from Disney. Christine's biggest dream was to be part of Disney's entertainment. More than anything, she wanted to be a character performer. Attractions and Bibbiti Bobbiti Boutique were also in her top roles, but overall entertainment was her ultimate goal. We talked about how I wanted to work in Hollywood Studios, and she told me about her audition for entertainment. She was the first really close friend I made through Tumblr, and we later grew closer through Facebook.

On September 18, 2012, I went through my normal routine of getting up early for school. I anxiously checked my email, hoping to see some sort of news from Disney waiting in my inbox. Several people had been receiving their acceptance emails over the past couple of days, which kept me at the edge of my seat whenever I logged on to my computer. Seeing all of these fellow applicants have their dreams come true was inspiring, but it also made me a little uneasy. Why hadn't I received any news yet? Where was my invitation to come work in Walt Disney World?

After another disappointing look into my inbox, I snatched my backpack and got in my car to start driving to class. As I crossed over my town's border and approached the freeway overpass, my phone started to ring. Odd, it's eight in the morning. Who would be calling me at such an early hour?

I glanced at my cell and noticed it was Sara. Assuming she was going to ask me a question about school, I answered and put her on speaker.

"What's up?"

"I GOT ACCEPTED!!!!" she shrieked.

My jaw dropped, "You WHAT?!"

"I'M OFFICIALLY DOING THE DISNEY COLLEGE PROGRAM!! I'm dancing around campus I'm so excited!"

My mind started racing, "Oh my gosh! I'm so happy for you!! What role did you get?"

"That's the funny part. I got quick service food and beverage." This was the one role we weren't really looking forward to doing, since it wasn't what we would expect to do when working at Walt Disney World. Nevertheless, Sara was thrilled.

The conversation ended quickly. since her early class was about to start. After we hung up, I pulled into a parking spot on campus. I was ecstatic for Sara, but her acceptance had me worried. She had her interview a day after mine, and was already accepted? She even didn't feel like she had done a good job during her interview and thought her interviewer wasn't impressed with her answers. I knew she was worrying about nothing and overthinking everything, so it wasn't a surprise that her assumptions were wrong. But why hadn't I heard back yet? Had I done something wrong?

Where was my acceptance?

CHAPTER SIX

The Moment of Truth

The next day I checked both my inbox and the Facebook group to see whether I had any news or whether anyone else was accepted that morning. Most of the acceptance waves occurred early in the day, so when I saw that no one had received any news yet, I assumed that this day wouldn't have any acceptances. Disappointed, I met up with Sara and endured another mundane day of computers and public speaking together.

While my professor was beginning to review what to expect the next day of class, I received a text from one of my Disney friends, Emily: "Have you checked your email? They're sending out acceptances right now!"

Under my desk I quickly replied, "Oh my gosh! No, I haven't! I'll check as soon as I'm done with class!"

"Okay, hurry! I didn't get an email yet, but definitely let me know if you did!"

The last five minutes seemed to go on forever, and I was half-tempted to just leave early to snag a computer in the library since I didn't have my laptop with me that day. As soon as the professor ended her lesson, I quickly said goodbye and jetted out the door. My stomach was fluttering with anticipation as I reached the student lounge and found a couple of my friends hanging out in a booth together. I rushed up to one of them and asked whether I could borrow his laptop. He said sure and I nearly died while waiting for the snail pace internet to log me into my email account. Finally, the website loaded and I noticed a beautiful red number one signaling that I had a new message in my inbox. My heart was pounding as I clicked on the purple envelope and waited for my inbox to open. As soon as the web page finished loading, I gasped.

Congratulations! You have been accepted into the Disney College Program for the Spring 2013 semester!

My dream officially came true. I squealed as I told my friends that I was accepted, and immediately clicked on the link to get more information about my acceptance and my role. After digging through several websites and pages, I noticed my role spelled out in bold letters: "You have been accepted for Quick Service Food and Beverage."

I couldn't help but laugh. At this point, I didn't even care that I hadn't originally wanted the role; all I could think about was that I was officially going to work in my favorite place in the entire world.

I hurriedly called my parents, who were simply ecstatic for me. I called Sara, but unfortunately she didn't answer. My friend Holly was in class already, so I sent her a text about the good news. I was telling everyone and anyone about my acceptance, I was just so incredibly excited! After receiving my congratulatory hug from Holly when she was finished with class, I drove back home blasting the radio and singing at the top of my lungs. When I got home, I literally fell on the carpet and rolled around with joy while on my way to my room. I skipped and danced around the kitchen and living room with a smile never leaving my face.

I'm officially a Disney cast member. This is the greatest day of my life.

CHAPTER SEVEN

Roommate Hunting

The next few weeks were a whirlwind of online paperwork, booking flights and hotels, creating a packing list, making new friends, finding roommates, and enduring the three months I had left at my community college. Sara and I also began to create a video blog series called Sara Squared DCP. In the videos, we shared our Disney bucket list and what we're packing, as well as a little about ourselves. We planned on filming our entire DCP experience to share with those interested in applying and to keep our family and friends back home updated on how we were doing in Florida. What we didn't realize was how many doors these videos would open to make new friends, which I will explain later.

The biggest project we needed to tackle was finding people to live with during the program. Unfortunately, our original plan to room with Katie, Giselle, Meriem, and Emily didn't work out, due to different arrival dates and role requirements. Also, finding roommates before getting accepted was not the best idea, since sadly Emily was not invited into program. (But there's good news for her! She was able to participate in the program right after ours!) Due to all of these obstacles, we had to start our roommate hunt from scratch. We reposted our roommate survey and scouted the Facebook group for girls who had similar interests and the same arrival date, and who wouldn't risk getting the rest of us in trouble for drinking. We would be placed in a wellness apartment, which did not allow any kind of alcohol. If someone was caught drinking or had signs of leftover bottles and cans from drinking, the entire apartment would be termed (fired) and immediately sent home. The last thing we wanted to worry about was getting termed for a roommate drinking in our apartment.

The first girl we connected with was Carmen. We had many similar interests and got along extremely well whenever we messaged each other over Facebook. Tumblr was a huge common interest between the two of us, and Sara and I decided she would be wonderful to have in our apartment. The only concern was that she was going to turn 21 during the first week of our program. She assured us that we wouldn't have to worry about her getting us in trouble with alcohol, and that she was fine living in a wellness apartment during her program.

Bethany was the next girl we talked to about rooming with all of us. She was also going to be working in quick service food and beverage and was majoring in marketing, just like me. We quickly invited her to be one of our roommates, and she said that she might know someone who would work well with the rest of us—Sarah (yes, a third girl with the same name). We all agreed she would be a wonderful addition to our apartment, so we invited her as well. With Bethany, Sarah, and Carmen as sure roommates, we just needed one more person to fill the three-bedroom apartment we all were hoping to get in Florida.

Finding our final roommate was a little trickier. I was talking to a girl named Samantha who actually lived pretty close to me, and we got along fairly well whenever we would text or message on Facebook. Once we found the other four girls, Samantha was the only one who wasn't completely committed to our apartment, since she was also talking to a few other girls who were inviting her to be their roommate. This was all completely fine; we understood that there was a possibility of her deciding on the other apartment instead of ours. However, as time went on, many of the promising candidates who had posted roommate surveys on the group page started to decide on their roommates, restricting our options if Samantaa didn't come with us.

We weren't too surprised when she decided to room with the other girls, so as soon as she told us, I scoured the Facebook groups to see whether there were any good candidates left. After a few failed attempts to find someone, I came across a very promising survey right before I was leaving for class; it was from a girl named Liz who had been accepted into merchandise. She had just posted her roommate survey and no one had commented on it yet. I immediately messaged her and quickly decided she would be perfect to include in our apartment. I messaged the other girls and let them talk to her a little bit while I was in school, and they all agreed that we wanted her to live with us. I'm so glad I was able to find her, because Liz became one of my closest and dearest friends during my program.

After everyone finally committed to rooming together, we needed to decide on an apartment complex from the four available. The oldest and most affordable complex is Vista Way, but we weren't interested in staying there due to its lack of three bedroom apartments and reputation for partying. The Commons is the most expensive apartment complex, mainly houses international students, and also doesn't have three bedrooms as an option, so we ruled it out, too. That left us with Patterson Court and Chatham Square. Patterson is the newest apartment complex, but Chatham is closest to the bus stop and not much older than Patterson. The price for rent was exactly the same for three bedroom apartments, but after watching multiple apartment tour videos online, we all agreed we were going to ask for Chatham Square. The close bus stop was just something we couldn't pass up.

The six of us were all so excited to have found each other. We all got along really well and kept in contact every once in a while to get to know one another better before moving to Florida. I talked to Carmen the most, with Bethany a close second. I was anxious to meet them in person in January, especially since they were going to be my first roommates when I left home.

Now all we needed to do was pass the time until January, when all of our dreams, in the best Disney fashion, would come true.

CHAPTER EIGHT

Disney Purgatory

We booked our flights to depart from Sacramento at 8:30 in the morning on January 7, 2013, with a layover in Las Vegas. With the flights scheduled and living situations set, focusing on our last couple months of school was like pulling teeth. Learning about weather patterns in physical geography seemed pointless now that I was going to work in the Happiest Place on Earth.

Whenever we weren't pining over textbooks and straining to pay attention to our professors in class, we spent as much time with our friends and family as possible before the big move. Every Wednesday, Sara and I went to the local café for a trivia night with our friends to escape the stress of school and responsibilities for a couple of hours. We would also host movie and game nights, staying up late with friends watching *The Avengers* or playing Apples to Apples until the late hours of the night.

After a successful week of finals, I bid my community college goodbye and switched into complete Disney mode. I continued to make new friends through the Facebook group, connect with other people who planned on uploading YouTube videos during their programs, and spend time with my family over the holidays. Whenever I would see a Disney commercial, my heart fluttered with joy and excitement for the months ahead. The time was almost here. It was like I could taste the Mickey Premium Bar waiting for me once I arrived next week.

I had never moved out of my house before, and so my mom helped me go shopping for supplies and clothes that I might need during my stay in Florida. Since I was flying and not driving, we had a limited amount of items I could bring without exceeding the weight limit for my suitcases. Space bags were a lifesaver when it came to packing. I was able to fit most of my clothes into a single suitcase, while my other bag contained mainly shoes, jackets, and bathroom accessories. We had a list on our apartment Facebook group for what everyone was going to bring, so we knew that Liz was in charge of the TV, Sarah was going to bring a blender, I was bringing the router for the internet, and so on.

We hosted our going-away party two days before we were scheduled to move to Florida. Over 20 people arrived at my house to spend time with Sara and me one last time. There were so many people that I hadn't seen or spent quality time with in a long while. One of my friends since middle school made the most amazing chocolate and Nutella cake (the Nutella was a surprise for me; I'm obsessed), and we probably broke a record for largest game of Apples to Apples ever played. It was an amazing night, and I'm blessed that I got to see everyone before my Disney experience.

My last day at home was spent with my family and my closest friends. We have this tradition to have a "Last Supper" at In-N-Out Burger before school starts or when someone is moving away. This was definitely appropriate in our case, since both Sara and I love In-N-Out and won't be able to have it until we returned to California in the summer (there are none in Florida). Saying goodbye to everyone wasn't easy, but nothing was as hard as saying goodbye to my best friend, Holly.

Holly and another friend, Grace, accompanied me to Target right after In-N-Out so I could buy some last minute essentials. We slowly walked back to my car and turned to each other with dread. I hugged Grace goodbye, and tears started rolling down my cheeks as soon as I looked at Holly. She's been my closest and dearest friend since sixth grade, and we've never lived more than an hour away from each other. Now I was about to live on the other side of the country, more than five hours away on a plane. I wasn't expecting to say goodbye to her in a Target parking lot, but the time had come and there was no stopping it. We gave each other the biggest hug we've had in a long time, and I reminded myself that this wasn't goodbye forever; I was coming back in only five months. We slowly pulled away and returned to our cars after a final goodbye.

As soon as I shut my door and pulled out of the parking lot, I started bawling. It was it hit me that I was leaving everything I knew and everyone I loved to move across the country. By the time I arrived at my house, I was a sobbing mess. I looked at my phone and noticed that Holly had sent me a text that said, "Well, I cried all the way home."

This only made me even more heartbroken to be leaving, but a few moments later I started to calm down and realize that this was for the best. I was about to live my dream, and to do that I needed to step out of my comfort zone.

I spent the rest of the night frantically packing and double-checking to make sure I was prepared for tomorrow. I managed to finish by eight o'clock. As soon as I was done, I sent a text to Sara asking how she was doing. She replied, "I'm doing puzzles..."

Of course. I should have known the queen of procrastination was doing everything except preparing for moving to the other side of the country the next morning.

My mom helped me gather all of my things into the car, and I said goodbye to my brother, two dogs, and adorable fluffy cat. My dad wanted me to wake him up the next morning before I left to say goodbye, so I tried my best to go to sleep. Of course, how could someone sleep when their dream was coming true the next day?

CHAPTER NINE

The Big Day

"We need more Dole Whip!"

I was surrounded by a swarm of guests in my tiny stand in Adventureland, frantically trying to figure out how to work the Dole Whip machine. My coworkers looked back at me with panicked expressions due to the high demand from guests, which made me even more anxious and nervous than I already was. Each of my Dole Whips had to be thrown out because they looked like pathetic flops, not beautifully crafted cones.

I spun around and noticed many of my high school friends were in the horde. Some of my best friends looked at me with squinted eyes and pursed lips. Time was ticking, and no one was happy with my performance.

Suddenly everyone stopped what they were doing and turned to one direction. Apparently, it was time to do the national anthem, which required dropping everything and saluting the flag. I put down the Dole Whip I was working on and turned to the flag, waiting for the music to start. However, when it began, it was different from what I expected. Maroon 5 started playing, and it all began to go fuzzy...

My eyes shot open and I looked at the clock. It was 4:45 in the morning. I flew out of bed as soon as I realized what was happening: Today I moved to Florida.

I couldn't wipe the smile off my face as I got dressed and packed my things into the car with my mom. The sun wasn't even up, but I was prepared for this day. I said goodbye to my dad and my pets, then picked up Sara and her mom at their house a few minutes away. Before we knew it, we were on the road to Sacramento, had checked in our bags in the airport, said goodbye to our moms, and boarded our plane. I managed not to cry, because I was more excited than sad.

While we had our layover in Las Vegas, we ran into a group of students who looked around our age. We discovered that they were

The Big Day   23

also flying to Florida for the DCP, and most of them were from BYU Idaho. One of them actually knew one of Sara's friends that went to the same school! I also ran into a girl I knew from my church group in high school who was also moving to Disney on the same day for the program. This is definitely a very small world!

We finally boarded our plane and prepared ourselves for the long five-hour flight ahead of us. Sara was kind enough to give me the window seat while she sat in the middle. Unfortunately, a really large man decided to sit next to her and take a sleeping medication to snooze throughout the entire flight. If either of us needed to use the restroom or wanted to get out to stretch a little, we were out of luck. At the very end of the flight, the man woke up and started telling us this crazy story about how his wife back home had been attacked and told us not to trust anyone, because we seemed like nice girls. It was definitely an awkward start to our first time living away from home. Thankfully, we were able to keep the conversation relatively short, because the pilot announced the beginning of our descent.

I looked out the window and was filled with glee. Even though all I could see were city lights from the night sky, it was the first time I was looking at Florida; I finally had a glimpse of my new home.

The plane landed with a thud and screeched to a halt. I was already sweating from the humidity change as Sara and I raced off to baggage claim. I checked my phone and noticed that our roommate Carmen's flight had actually landed at the same time as ours. She joined us as we gathered our bags and climbed into the shuttle that took us to our hotel. We were staying in a Holiday Inn right next to Vista Way. Many people in the college program stayed the night here because it's walking distance to the check-in location, which was convenient for people like us who unfortunately didn't have cars. In fact, to prove how often future college program cast members stayed in this hotel, the shuttle driver asked us if we were participating in the DCP. He was disappointed when we said we weren't planning on staying in Vista Way, but it was still pretty funny to have him figure out why three college girls were staying at this specific hotel.

We arrived at the Holiday Inn, got our room keys, and plopped onto our beds. Flying for over five hours and losing three hours with time zone changes can really suck the energy out of you. However, our other three roommates were staying in the same hotel, and we really wanted to meet them as soon as possible. Bethany was the first person to join us in our room, and actually decided to stay the night with us instead of with her dad. The four of us went down to the Applebee's connected to the hotel to meet up with Lizzie and have dinner, with Sarah joining a little bit later. We all got along well right off the bat—a good thing, since we were going to be stuck with each other for the next five months!

After changing our minds way too many times, we finally decided to wake up at 3:30 in the morning the following day to walk over to Vista Way around four to wait in line for check-in. We left the restaurant around ten, but our energy kept most of us awake until 1:30. Needless to say, we were running on only two hours of sleep before we were up and ready to wait in line across the street.

When we arrived at Vista Way, there were only about 20 people in front of us. At first we were relieved; it seemed like we had a good chance at getting the apartment complex we wanted. Unfortunately, as the morning wore on, we realized that many of the people in front of us were actually saving their spots in line for the rest of their roommates who were either sleeping in or arriving from a long distance away. Because of this, the amount of people in front of us grew dramatically within just a couple hours.

At around 6:30, three of us decided to walk to Walgreens across the street to get food and water. We had been waiting in line for almost three hours, and the lack of sleep was starting to creep up on some of us. About a half an hour later, the people in charge of check-in decided to move our line up onto Vista property, so that we weren't snaking all the around the block. By this time I started recognizing some faces from the Facebook group, which was definitely strange to experience. Not too far behind us was Samantha, the girl who was almost our roommate but who had decided to go with some other girls. Coincidentally, she ended up rooming with a girl from my town who I knew from a church group I used to attend while in high school.

At 7:30, they led us to a main building with some canopies where we waited for a little bit before they formally checked us into the system, making sure they had our correct email addresses and phone numbers. After this, we received our brand-new, official Disney College Program planner book, which was soon going to reveal where we were all working on Disney property. Butterflies fluttered in my stomach as I slowly crept forward in line. One by one, my roommates discovered where they were going to be working for the next five months.

Sara was first. We all held our breath while we waited for her results. The man asked for her name, then placed a sticker on her planner, which revealed her location: the Roaring Fork in the Wilderness Lodge. Neither of us had ever been to this hotel (or to any Walt Disney World resort). Then again, Sara had never been to Walt Disney World at all, so she was happy with any location.

I was next. I took a hesitant step forward as the man asked for my name. He found my label and placed the sticker on my notebook. With my fingers crossed, I prayed over and over again to see Hollywood Studios or Magic Kingdom on that little piece of paper. I swallowed as I looked down at the bold writing: Capt. Cook's in the Polynesian Resort. My heart sank a little. The man told me it was a beautiful hotel, but I wasn't sure how I felt about not being in a park. Whenever I pictured myself doing the program, I always imagined helping guests in one of the main for theme parks. I hadn't even considered the possibility of working in a hotel, much less one I'd never seen before.

I pushed a smile on my face and thanked the man, while we discovered where the rest of our roommates were going to be working. Bethany was placed in the food court in DisneyQuest in Downtown Disney, Liz would be on Main Street in Magic Kingdom, Carmen in the Contemporary Resort, and Sarah was going to be a safari tour guide for Kilimanjaro Safaris in Animal Kingdom. We were all excited to discover where we would be working, but after this initial excitement came paperwork, paperwork, and even more paperwork. I was starting to wish I had brought a folder, because all of my personal copies of the documents I had to sign became a handful, almost slipping through my arms a few times while waiting in all the various lines.

Once we were finished with everything outside, we walked into the main building to at last request an apartment complex. We excitedly skipped up to the open cast member in charge of apartment placement and anxiously requested a three bedroom in Chatham Square. After a quick search through her computer, she regretted to inform us that the group in front of us took the last one available. We all froze. Where were we all going to agree on living now? But the woman was nice and gave us two similar options: either we can stay in Chatham and add two random roommates for a four-bedroom apartment, or we can switch to Patterson Court and keep all of the same roommates.

We quickly agreed on Patterson, and then went to take photos for our housing IDs. I looked like a serial killer thanks to the humidity's effect on my hair and sleep deprivation. At that point, I just wanted my new bed. Unfortunately, we still had to take a bus to Casting to do even more paperwork and get information about our training schedules, as well as get our fingerprints taken and learn about our work location. The most exciting part of this portion of the day was when we were on the bus about to drive onto Disney property for the first time. The cast member with the microphone was quizzing us Disney trivia questions, and asked us to all count down in unison as we were about to drive under the "Welcome to the Walt Disney World Resort" sign. Everyone cheered as we entered Disney, and in that moment I realized I was finally living my dream.

After finishing the endless amounts of paperwork, we boarded one final bus back to Vista Way, gathered our things to check out from the hotel, and drove to our new apartment. It was beautiful! Our apartment was on the second floor, right next to the pool, clubhouse, gym, and laundry room. Before we unpacked, Sara and I immediately crashed on our beds and took a nap. Two hours of sleep, massive jet lag, and a really long morning filled with walking and standing hit us hard by the time we were in our apartment. Turns out, while we were sleeping our friends Katie and Giselle knocked on our door (the two best friends we almost roomed with). Their apartment was right below ours!

We all ended the night with our first (and last) trip to Walmart. There were so many tourists and college program participants shopping at the same time that we were overwhelmed. Sara and I bought the most adorable comforters for our beds; they matched our personalities perfectly. Mine was black with purple and pink peace signs all over, while Sara's was white with pink and green flowers. After our chaotic trip to Walmart, we decorated our rooms to make them look livable and crashed in our new beds for the night.

I can safely say that this first full day in Florida was the most exhausting of my life. Conquering check-in, filling in mountains of paperwork at Casting, moving into my first apartment, meeting new friends, shopping, and unpacking, all on only two hours of sleep, was just the start of this crazy and exciting journey ahead. It was now full speed toward our new lives working for Disney, and we were more than ready to officially start our adventure of a lifetime tomorrow.

CHAPTER TEN

Resort Hopping

We had the next couple days off to explore the area around the apartment, go grocery shopping (there was a Super Target a few blocks away, which made me happy), and spend time with my roommates to get to know each other. I learned that Sarah was the most talkative, Bethany was incredibly sweet, and Carmen and Liz were a little quieter. We were all excited for Traditions so we could visit the parks together. It was difficult to decide which park to visit first, but I knew that I needed to see Hollywood Studios as soon as possible. Rock 'n' Roller Coaster and Tower of Terror were calling my name.

A few days after moving in, we had our mandatory housing meeting. Everyone who had the same arrival date as us needed to assemble in The Commons down the street for a meeting about all of Disney's housing policies, such as curfews, guests, and what to expect during inspections. Some people who went the meeting the day before warned us that it was going to be boring, but it wasn't that bad. They played the soundtracks from *High School Musical* and *Camp Rock* before the meeting, which made up for all the dull moments later on.

As soon as the meeting finished, my roommates decided to hop on a bus and explore some of our work locations at the resorts. Sara and I had never experienced any Disney resorts in Florida, so we were excited to see where we were going to be working.

Our first stop was at the Polynesian. As we tried to find our way around the massive resort, I fell in love with the landscaping and the overall theme. The large tropical shrubs, beautiful flowers, and palm trees made me feel like I had just stepped into paradise. We walked through the main lobby doors and I was blown away. The waterfall in the middle of the room, with flowers and plants towering above it, was breathtaking. We walked around as I took everything in and tried to register that I'd be working here for the next five months.

Down the hall we passed a beautiful Wyland photo gallery store, turned the corner, and saw my restaurant: Capt. Cook's.

We decided that Capt. Cook's would be a good place to eat, since I wanted to know what kind of food I would be selling and we didn't know what the food options would be like in the other resorts. On the right side of the room we ordered on a touch screen menu, which was something I've never experienced before. I chose the chicken stir-fry and went to the cashier to pay. I told her that I was going to be working there and she smiled and asked if I was doing the program. I told her yes and that I'd start training next week, but also asked where I would be meeting for orientation. (All my information paper said was "The Tikki Room", which I knew wasn't the popular attraction in Magic Kingdom.) As she took care of my transaction, she tried to explain where the room was and gave me my pager for my order. Her directions didn't make a whole lot of sense, so I just thanked her and joined my roommates to wait for my food.

After we ate, we decided it was time to finally try Dole Whip. I had never tried it before, but I had heard all the hype from talking to other Disney fans. For those of you who don't know what Dole Whip is, it's a pineapple soft-serve ice cream, similar to fruit-flavored sherbet. I knew I'd probably like it because I love pineapple, but I wasn't expecting it to taste so heavenly. After the first bite, I was hooked. It was going to be very dangerous selling Dole Whip for the next five months.

We finished our Dole Whips and then hopped on the monorail to the next stop, the Contemporary, where Carmen was going to be working. There wasn't much to explore in this resort in comparison to the Polynesian, so we ended up hanging out in the gift shop and taking fun pictures will all the ridiculous Disney hats they had for sale.

Afterward, we had to find a way to get to the Wilderness Lodge, where Sara was assigned. Since her resort was the only one near Magic Kingdom with no monorail, we had to first stop at the theme park and take a bus from the there to Wilderness Lodge. I became obsessed with her resort. The buildings all look like giant cabins with pine trees around them. The main lobby has a huge fireplace with rocking chairs and a geyser that goes off every so often. Outside near the lake there's a waterfall that trickles down into the pool. It reminded me of where my family would go camping in the summer, which made me miss home for the first time.

We were able to find Sara's restaurant, The Roaring Fork, but decided it was time to call it a night. Both Sara and Carmen had Traditions early the next morning, so we hopped on a CP bus and headed back to the apartments. While we were on the bus I had time to really reflect about my situation. I had been disappointed with my role, not being able to live in Chatham, and not being able to work in a theme park. But after visiting the Polynesian and exploring the other resorts, I realized just how perfect my hotel was for me. I adore tropical beaches, sunshine, and summer, so I knew I was going to appreciate working at the Polynesian.

Back at the apartment, I couldn't wait until tomorrow, when I would become an official Disney cast member, and at last get to explore the parks!

CHAPTER ELEVEN

Welcome to the Disney Family

Every Disney cast member must go through an orientation process called Traditions. Sara and Carmen had the early morning session, and the rest of us were lucky enough to sleep in for the afternoon class. One advantage for the morning class was that they had the rest of their day to spend in the parks if they wished, while everyone in the afternoon class would barely have an hour or so of free time before the parks closed.

Everyone attending Traditions must dress professionally and meet the Disney Look guidelines. Many people are unsure of what the "Disney Look" means, but I usually just tell them to dress as if they're going to a job interview.

I had heard a variety of stories about Traditions. The range of opinions spanned from indifferent and slightly boring, to incredibly emotional. Some cast members apparently even started crying near the end. I was nervous about what to expect. I had no idea what was going to happen when we hopped onto a massive bus and arrived at Disney University for our class.

The cast members in charge arranged us into different sections and ushered us into various classrooms. Bethany was in my group, so I wasn't as lost and alone in a sea of brand-new college program participants. After sitting in our seats and casually chatting with the other people at our table, Traditions began.

The facilitators welcomed us to the Disney family, explaining the basic outline for what we should expect for the rest of the day. We started with a few welcome videos and then learned the differences between working for Disney and a different company. Here at Disney, we're called "cast members", and our main job is to "perform in the show" no matter where you're working in Disney World. You have the power to create magic and memories that can last a lifetime for any guests or families you might meet during their vacation.

To fully understand our role with the show and the origins of where we were going to be working, we needed to learn all about how everything started: with a man named Walt Disney.

Instead of simply teaching and lecturing us about Walt's life and history, our lesson started with a game. Every table was given snapshots of different moments in Disney history, starting with Walt's birth and early life all the way to the most recent years. Our job was to do our best to place each snapshot in the correct chronological order. I've always loved researching Walt's life, so the first half of the game was rather easy to put together. My group had a little more trouble with the second half of the timeline, but we fared rather well. We didn't win for most accurate, but it was still fun!

As we corrected our timelines, we learned all about the details of each landmark in Disney history—from Disney's first fully animated Technicolor movie, *Snow White and the Seven Dwarfs*, to the conception and creation of Disneyland, all the way to the present day with Pixar movies and the creation of Disney Cruise Line. I always love learning more about Walt's life and Disney history as a whole, so I enjoyed this portion of our orientation.

Along with knowing the history of the company, it was also important for us to learn about the "Four Keys" that create the basis of excellent customer service at Disney. In order of importance, cast members must always be aware and use safety, courtesy, show (presentation), and efficiency.

"As long as you keep these Four Keys in mind while you work, you will have a successful experience when working here at Disney," one of our facilitators explained. "In fact, would you like to see these Four Keys in action right now?"

The room buzzed with excitement and anticipation over what he was going to say next: "Let's take a field trip to Magic Kingdom and see the Four Keys firsthand!"

Everyone was jumping out of their seats and incredibly excited to finally see Magic Kingdom after the long days of moving and checking in. I was excited to get out of the classroom after sitting for a few hours. We gathered together into buses and made our way to the park. Once we walked on stage, one of the facilitators asked whether it was anyone's first time in Magic Kingdom. A few hands shot into the air, and he encouraged them to come to the front of the group for the best view during the tour.

The trip down Main Street and near the castle was rather quick, but throughout our mini-excursion we were asked to identify where the different Keys were utilized around the park. For example, the sidewalks were painted a different color than the walkway to indicate a higher ground so people would notice for safety. All cast members had neat, clean, and appropriately themed costumes for show. While I was participating in the activity, I was soaking in the fact that I was walking down Main Street for the first time as a Disney cast member. I had also almost forgotten how much bigger Magic Kingdom was compared to Disneyland, especially the castle. Cinderella Castle was absolutely beautiful.

We made our way back to our Traditions classroom after the quick tour so the facilitators could explain a few more basic facts and information that we should know before we started working. After all questions were answered, we watched a video filled with cast members welcoming us to the Disney family. As the video played, I started to grow a little teary-eyed that I was finally a Disney cast member. I had dreamed about this for a long time; it was incredible that it was coming true.

Everyone was bustling with excitement as we exited and received our official cast IDs and nametags. We could all tell that this was going to be one incredible adventure. I was more than ready to be a part of it.

CHAPTER TWELVE

First Days of Park Fun

The following morning I woke up with a smile on my face and a spark of happiness in my heart. Today I was going back to Disney World for the first time in nearly five years.

All of my roommates except Bethany had the day off, so the five of us went to play in the parks for the first time as Disney cast members. I was excited that we were starting in Hollywood Studios, my favorite park out of the four. After exploring Studios, we were going to end our night in Magic Kingdom.

Sara, Carmen, and I caught a bus for Hollywood Studios first. Liz was driving Sarah a little later, so the three of us decided to get a head start. After numerous bus stops (we wondered if we were ever going to make it), we finally arrived. I could hardly contain my excitement as I checked in through security and gazed upon the beautiful blue entrance. I skipped toward the entrance and scanned my ID to enter a Disney park as a cast member.

I squealed as we walked toward Mickey's giant sorcerer hat in the middle of the street. I kept an eye on Sara to see her reactions, since this was her first time in Hollywood Studios. Before we did any attractions, we took a quick detour to a gift shop so Carmen could purchase some birthday Mickey ears. With her new hat snug on her head, the three of us knew exactly which ride to conquer first: Tower of Terror.

We raced through tourists and families down Sunset Boulevard with the beautiful haunted hotel in our view. This is one of my all-time favorite rides at both Disney World and Disneyland. It was the perfect way to kick-start my incredible journey as a cast member.

One reason why I'm obsessed with Tower of Terror is the theme. The moment you walk into the abandoned hotel lobby, you know you're entering a story. Cobwebs are draped along the dusty chandeliers, while lamps and figurines look as if they haven't been touched in decades. A bellhop looms gloomily over his or her podium, glaring at the guests as they make their way to the library doors. Once inside the spooky library, you can hear thunder and see lightning flashing through the cracked windows. Before you know it, the lights go out and you're now paying close attention to a black-and-white screen explaining the story behind the Hollywood Tower Hotel.

"Hollywood, 1939..."

After the video, you walk outside the library to find yourself in the boiler room to board the awaiting maintenance service elevator, its door ominously open. Once inside with seatbelts buckled, another bellhop wishes you luck, and you're sent into the next dimension. There's no turning back.

This is my absolute favorite part. As soon as you're whisked away to the top, you're quickly dropping 13 stories at various speeds. Every ride is different, and with each drop my stomach soars and flutters with butterflies and cheerful and terrified screams shrill throughout the elevator. It's one of the most thrilling and exciting feelings to experience in Disney, and it's something that will never grow old for me.

Once we stepped off our elevator and exited the attraction, Sarah and Liz arrived at the parks. We met each other outside of Tower of Terror and decided to ride another of my favorites, Aerosmith's Rock 'n' Roller Coaster. Liz chose to sit out on this one, but my thrill crave was only hungrier after experiencing Tower. The coaster takes off at a lightning speed, from zero to 60 miles per hour in a matter of seconds. With three inversions and Aerosmith music blasting in your ears, this attraction never fails to plaster a smile on my face.

We reunited with Liz afterwards and went to meet some characters. I was excited to find Wreck-It Ralph and Venollope Von Schweetz from *Wreck-It Ralph*, who were only recently introduced into the Disney family. Meeting characters was something rather new for me, since I was too shy and rather terrified of them when I was younger.

To my surprise, as we entered the Animation Academy, I was greeted by two of my all time favorite characters from my favorite Pixar movie: Mr. Incredible and Frozone from *The Incredibles*. I'm not joking when I say this is one of my favorite films. I can recite almost all the dialogue when I'm watching it at home. It annoys my friends, but it's become such a habit that I don't even notice that I'm doing it anymore.

To my delight, there was hardly anyone in line for the two super heroes. Sara and I quickly made it to the front and Frozone motioned for us to come over and meet them. I asked them to sign my brand-new autograph book and then prepared to pose for a photo. Frozone asked Sara to flex, and quivered in fear at the sight of her "muscles". Mr. Incredible had me put my hands on my hips like a brave superhero right before we took the picture. Meeting them couldn't have been more perfect for my first character experience during my program.

Waiting for Wreck-It Ralph and Vanellope took a little longer, which made sense since the movie had just been released in theaters. We took a group photo with them and moved on to the Great Movie Ride before heading to Magic Kingdom.

I had forgotten how massive Magic Kingdom is in comparison to Disneyland. I was so used to Disneyland at this point in my life that I was a little discombobulated while walking through this massive park. Even Main Street is bigger in scale than the original in Disneyland, and don't get me started on the castle. Aurora's castle in Anaheim is miniscule compared to Cinderella's in Orlando. Aurora's has its charms, but Cinderella's is absolutely breathtaking. All of the lands are completely different as well. There's no New Orleans Square or Critter Country, and Magic Kingdom's New Fantasyland was completely different than the one in California. Toontown is no longer in Disney World; in its place I found Storybook Circus where you can ride Dumbo and meet characters like Minnie Mouse and Goofy in their circus outfits.

Tomorrowland is different, too. Disneyland's version is rather out of date since removing the PeopleMover, while Florida's is much grander in scale. There are more attractions and places to eat in the Magic Kingdom Tomorrowland; in fact, Cosmic Rays became my go-to place for lunch or dinner with Liz throughout our program.

However, Pirates of the Caribbean and Space Mountain are two of my favorite attractions in Disneyland, and their Florida counterparts just can't compare. For some reason, they took out certain scenes and shortened the Pirates ride in Florida, while Space Mountain needs a massive refurbishment and update. It's extremely jerky and uncomfortable, which is why I only went on it a handful of times.

The five of us hopped on board a few rides such as Pirates, Haunted Mansion, and the Little Mermaid attraction in New Fantasyland. At the end of the night, Bethany joined us and we all found a spot in front of the castle to watch the nighttime spectaculars for my first time. I quickly fell in love with Celebrate the Magic, a projection show on the castle performed before the fireworks and the electric parade. Wishes, the fireworks show, was absolutely breathtaking. I hadn't sat and watched the fireworks in a Disney park since before I can remember, and I was filled with overwhelming emotion reflecting where I was at that point in my life and how lucky I was to be living my dream as part of the Disney family.

After the fireworks, we took a roommate photo together in front of the castle and then found a perfect spot to watch the Main Street Electric Parade. I've never seen this parade, but I remember listening to the music on a Disneyland cassette tape when I was little. It was cool to finally see it in person after hearing the audio many times when I was so young. My favorite part was (and still is) the Pinocchio float, especially the donkey boys dancing around, scaring guests, and making silly faces to everyone along the parade route.

Overall, the entire day in the parks was perfect. I couldn't wait to continue my journey and explore the parks even more over the next five months. But first, Disney needed to put me to work.

CHAPTER THIRTEEN

Aloha!

I woke up bright and early the following Monday to take a bus back to Disney University for my first official day of training. Each department in Disney has its own class at Disney University before beginning their training in their park or resort. For example, those involved in Entertainment or PhotoPass must take "Welcome to Entertainment". The class I attended was called "Food and Beverage Core Café", which is a class everyone in foods must take whether in a park or a resort. This includes cast members involved with table service restaurants, quick service restaurants, outdoor food carts, and culinary.

In this class, we learned all about food safety and health hazards. For example, they explained proper temperatures to maintain certain types of food, as well as how to properly wash your hands and use gloves. It was a little difficult to keep track of all the different temperatures and safety instructions, but it also didn't help that I'm not a morning person and the class started at 8:30 am.

After watching numerous food safety videos and having Disney's safety motto "Safe-D Begins with Me!" engrained into my brain, I was happy to go back to my apartment and relax for the rest of the afternoon.

My first official day at the Polynesian was called "Aloha Day". I wasn't quite sure where to meet for this orientation, so I decided to take the earlier bus that arrived at the resort around an hour before my start time. There was hardly anyone on the B bus that morning, but I was grateful to see another girl get off at the Polynesian stop with me. We were both attending Aloha Day and had left super early to make sure we could find the meeting location.

The two of us walked to the main lobby together and introduced ourselves. I learned that she was an International College Program student from Australia. She was going to be a hostess at 'Ohana, the table service restaurant located right above my little food court.

Since she was an ICP, she was scheduled to work in Disney World for a full year. The difference between ICPs and those participating in my program is that halfway through her program she was to switch roles and work in a different location. I was jealous of this opportunity, since I'd love to work in various places in the parks or other resorts and gain experience in different roles.

After asking a few front desk cast members for help, we finally found our location and took a seat at a long table. We were the first ones to arrive and soon learned that many of the others who came on the bus after us were just as lost as we had been. I was excited to see my friend Lindsey from Tumblr at orientation with me. She was going to work as a hostess in Kona Café upstairs.

Once everyone arrived, our orientation leader passed out pamphlets with information about the Polynesian Resort. We were taught that the Polynesian was one of the first resorts to open in Walt Disney World along with the Magic Kingdom in 1971. The Polynesian captures the beauty and magic of both Disney and the Polynesian Isles. All cast members are considered each other's family, or "ohana", within the resort. Just as Lilo explained to Stitch, "Ohana means family, and family means no one gets left behind…or forgotten."

There are three table service restaurants in the Polynesian: 'Ohana, Kona Café, and the Spirit of Aloha, which is an outdoor show filled with Polynesian dancing and delicious food. Capt. Cook's, where I was going to work, was the only quick service food court in the resort. There are eleven longhouses, each named after a Polynesian island, such as Fiji, Tahiti, and Rapa Nui. The main lobby and reception area is called the Great Ceremonial House, with access to the monorail, the bus stop, and numerous gift shops. The Polynesian is also home to the "Nanea" (tranquil) volcano pool, which features a water slide and underwater music.

We took a tour of the entire resort to learn about its history in detail while experiencing it first hand. Whenever we walked by a guest or fellow cast member, our orientation leader would say, "Aloha!" as a greeting. This quickly became my way of saying hi to all of the guests I encountered while working in the Polynesian; it sometimes accidentally slipped out even when I wasn't on duty.

Once we finished the general orientation for the resort, we were split into groups according to our work location and role. There was one other cast member (a Hawaiian, appropriately enough!) from the college program that was going to be working with me in Capt. Cook's. One of the trainers from our restaurant gave us menus to look over. The two of us had no idea what was going to happen next. It turned out to be a demanding drill-and-memorization exercise to learn and remember all the food options on the menu.

Our trainer had us break off each section of the menu into parts, labeling them with letters and numbers. She'd have us study certain sections for about thirty seconds, flip over the menu, and fire question after question at us about that section. She'd ask us the various options for flatbreads, what's included in the Polynesian salad, what are the vegetarian options, what's offered for children on the breakfast menu, and more. I was surprised with how much I was able to memorize in such a short amount of time. It was a stressful and demanding technique, but it really worked and helped when it came to recalling the menu for guests and answering their questions.

The next couple days of training consisted of learning on the computer. These days seemed to drag on forever...long eight-hour shifts in front of a computer screen learning all about the Disney Dining Plan and how to work a cash register weren't tremendously exciting. The Dining Plan was the most confusing aspect, since I had never heard about it before. Basically, guests that stay in a Disney resort have the option to pre-pay for a certain amount of quick service and table service meals, along with a specific number of snacks during their trip. Quick service meals come with an entrée, drink, and dessert every single time, and each guest is allowed one refillable mug to use at their hotel whenever they please throughout their vacation. Explaining this dining plan to guests became one of the core parts of my job, which means it was vital to understand every aspect of the plan to dispel any confusion that guests might have (which was a lot).

After our last day of training on the computers, we were allowed to get our costumes. I was excited to see what mine looked like, since Disney costumes have a reputation for being fun and cute to fit the location's theme. I was thinking I was going to wear something tropical, noticing lots of floral print on other costumes such as the front desk receptionists and the custodial cast members. I brainstormed all the possibilities in my head while we walked across the street to Costuming. Once we arrived, our trainer pointed us to the costumes for our restaurant. As soon as I saw what I was going to be wearing, I almost laughed.

My costume was hideous.

I know some people may argue that they have the worst costume, but I can sincerely assure you that what I had to wear for the next five months was the worst costume I've ever seen. The pants and apron were a dull orange color, while the shirt looked like a really tacky wallpaper pattern from the 1970s. It had what seemed like leaves from tropical plants in different shades of green with dark orange accents within the brush. Later, Sara actually found a chair in a condo with the same exact print. All of my coworkers found it hilarious to know that we were wearing the same print as a piece of furniture.

I took my costume home to compare it to those of my roommates. Sarah's safari costume was adorable, resembling an African tour guide. She even had hiking boots! Lizzie had two different costumes for her locations on Main Street, which consisted of a yellow dress with an apron and chef/bakery hat, as well as an outfit with a classy blouse, tie, and long skirt. Sara looked like a little lumberjack in her plaid shirt and red apron for the Wilderness Lodge. Carmen had a very professional costume for the Contemporary Resort, with a simple blue blouse and gray slacks. Bethany's costume for DisneyQuest had a variety of neon colors to match the video game heaven in Downtown Disney.

It was exciting to hear about my roommates' experiences during training. Even though some of us were in the same roles, everyone was going through a different process. Sara's on-the-job training was going to last over two weeks, while mine was only five days. Sarah had to memorize a 30-minute spiel about animals and learn to drive a giant truck filled with guests. However, we couldn't talk too late into the night, because I had my first day of on-the-job training in Capt. Cook's the next morning. I was nervous yet excited to finally see what I would be doing in my restaurant. I was getting used to waking up at the crack of dawn to catch a bus and work for eight hours.

CHAPTER FOURTEEN

Learning the Ropes

"Do you have a jacket?"

This was the first thing my trainer asked me on day one of my on-the-job training. The initial position I was going to learn was the stocker. Stocking was very simple and straightforward. My trainer showed me where all of the extra food and drink supplies were kept, taught me how to restock the cooler that stored all of our drinks and refrigerated snacks, as well as where all of the chemicals and emergency exits were located in the food court and nearby in the resort.

One of the best parts about training was the free food. I was lucky to be at a restaurant that allowed its cast members in training to try the food before selling it to the guests. This way, we would all know what the food tasted like, our preferences, and what we can recommend to other people, as well as help us remember the ingredients for each item on the menu. My first day of tasting involved the chicken sandwich and Caesar salad. I couldn't even finish it all; it was way too much food!

My second day of training was for the counter position, and it became my favorite role. I was constantly busy doing something and the time flew by. This is one place where knowing the ingredients to the entrees is extremely helpful. At counter, I was in charge of preparing orders for guests after the culinary team cooked the food. I would look at the guest's receipt for their order, grab the food in the window, add any necessary sides such as fries, soup, or vegetables, then page the guest to come and pick up their food. This is where I learned that Capt. Cook's is extremely busy in the morning, especially on a Saturday during a three-day weekend when I was training. We became backed up in the middle of the morning for breakfast, but my trainer and manager both helped me learn the ropes during the hectic rush, and we were able to have a much more steady and manageable crowd once the afternoon began and we started serving lunch.

My third day of training was for the most challenging position: cashier. It was the first time I had ever worked with an actual cash register, so I was nervous about doing well. Disney's cash registers are completely touch screen, and have many buttons, options, and menus to search through to find specific products. We learned the basics about using their cash registers during my training on the computers, but actually using them was a completely different story.

For the first few hours I simply stood next to my trainer and observed her interacting with guests and using the point-of-sale system. I learn best by watching other people, so it took just a little while before I felt comfortable enough to step in and try it first hand. After greeting the guest, I needed to scan the receipt for their order. If the guest had the Disney Dining Plan or simply wanted to add some snack items or drinks, I had to find them on my computer manually and add them to the order. This was when my knowledge of the Disney Dining Plan was put to the test. I had to ask my trainer quite a few times to help clarify the process and the plan for the guests whenever they were confused. I also could not remember to apply a pager number to each order before pushing the "total" button. After I push total, the order is sent back as a receipt to the person at the counter. If there's no pager number on the order, the counter cast member has to call the cashier back to see if they remember which number was applied to a specific order. I started to feel more comfortable with the dining plan, giving back change, and the entire cashier process after a couple hours of practice. Thankfully, I had another day dedicated to this role just to make sure I felt confident enough in my abilities before tackling it on my own after training.

The second day at cashier was much better than the first. This time, I was working solely in the afternoon with the lunch and dinner menu, unlike breakfast the day before. Since I already had the basic idea of how the role worked, I immediately jumped into position when I started training. At first, I was once again having a difficult time remembering to add pagers to orders, but by the end of the night I was making sure to enter the numbers first thing when the guests came to pay for their food so that I wouldn't forget.

This is when I learned that I prefer afternoon instead of morning shifts. Not only do I not have to wake up at four or five in the morning to catch an insanely early bus, but the crowds are much more calm and manageable in the restaurant. Of course, there's a dinner rush around five or six, as well as a pre-fireworks rush when every guest buys Dole Whip and takes it out to watch Wishes on the beach, but it isn't as insane as the breakfast crowd.

A couple of days before my afternoon cashier training shift I went to Magic Kingdom with a few of my roommates and ate at Casey's Corner on Main Street. Eating there and experiencing the chaos that comes with working a quick service restaurant in a theme park definitely made me appreciate my location at the Polynesian. Casey's (and many other park restaurants) gets ridiculously busy. I don't know if I would have been able to handle that much of a crowd rush on such a constant basis in comparison to the languid Capt. Cook's.

At the end of my final cashier-training shift, my trainer showed me how to close out the cash register and count the money to make sure we came out even at the end of the night. The cashiers were always responsible for this task while we prepared to transition to our third shift phase for the rest of the night. Since Capt. Cook's is open 24 hours, after our regular day-shift cast members "closed", a couple of us had to stay later to prepare the restaurant for the cast member who was going to be in charge of working for the rest of the night. I was glad that college program cast members weren't required to learn the third shift position. This was usually only for full time and every once in a while part time cast members who agreed to do it.

My fifth and final day of training seemed to never end. I was an AmBUSSador, which is a fancy term for someone in charge of bussing tables and keeping the restaurant clean. The job was easy, and we had one more person than usual doing the job because I was training and was technically "shadowing" my trainer. However, the person who was in charge of scheduling made a mistake, which led to my trainer starting his shift two hours before me, leaving our breaks at different times. As a result, I was on my own during the majority of my shift, which wasn't bad because there wasn't too much to learn at this position. The majority of my job was keeping the condiments bar (napkins, utensils, etc.) stocked, cleaning tables, and making sure the dining room and patio area were neat and organized. If I was assigned the beverage side of the restaurant, I was also in charge of cleaning the drink machines at the end of the night. It's not a tough job, but it was a nice change of pace because we were extremely slow that night.

One huge downfall of my last day of training: my shift lasted until 1:30 in the morning, even though I didn't have much to do so late besides restocking napkins and bussing a few tables for the last two hours of my shift; hardly anyone comes into the restaurant after midnight.

By the time 1:30 rolled around, I was more than ready to head back to my apartment and sleep for the rest of my life. I was the only one on the bus back home, which was a long 40-minute drive since the Polynesian was the first stop on the entire route. I was drifting off during most of the drive and felt relieved when we finally made it back to the Chatham bus stop. After five days of training, my feet were in so much pain that the short walk back to my apartment seemed to take forever. Once I made it to Patterson, I trudged up the stairs, entered my apartment, and plopped into bed. I was so happy training was over and that I had the next two days off. Working 30–40 hours a week was going to take some adjustments, both for my stamina and my poor aching feet.

CHAPTER FIFTEEN

On My Own

I had the next two days off after training. Of course, instead of taking those days to rest and recover from all of the long shifts, I hung out in Hollywood Studios and Magic Kingdom with a few of my roommates each day. After my time off, the following day consisted simply of a four-hour class about safety in the work place, which allowed me the rest of the day to relax and prepare myself for my first shifts without a trainer.

I was at the counter during my first shift on my own. It was my luck that this day happened to be one of the busiest days the restaurant had seen in a while. Attempting to maintain a steady yet quick pace with keeping track of all the orders and paging the guests within a reasonable amount of time was a handful. When the restaurant is busy, many orders appear at the same time, which is rather overwhelming when you're new and not quite used to the process. My manager helped me during the dinner rush and reminded me that I needed to also take care of the baking area and make sure it was fully stocked. I was happy she told me because I thought I only had to stock the baking area on stocking day, not when I was at the counter.

When orders start piling up, I would apparently get a stressed and worried look on my face because the chefs kept asking me if I was okay. I was a little frazzled with the immense number of guests during my first day on my own, but overall I handled it rather well. I soon learned that I really enjoy a fast-paced work environment, because it requires you to stay busy and the time goes by quickly.

The rest of the work week I was mainly on counter, with one day as the breaker. The breaker is rather self-explanatory: this person is in charge of giving everyone breaks throughout the day. At the beginning of the shift, we all have a meeting with our manager to see what we need to focus on during the day, whether there have been any changes in the restaurant or food, as well as confirm who had what position for the rest of the night. This was also when the breaker received a list of everyone's breaks so they knew when to go to certain positions and for how long each break would last. I enjoyed this role because I bounced around from both cash registers to the counter throughout the day, giving me a good variety during my shift. I felt a great sense of accomplishment when I was able to go through two hours at both cashiers without forgetting a single pager!

One of my managers was impressed with how well I was able to manage the counter without stressing or falling behind, even though I was still so new. Another day the same manager also complimented me on how well I kept the bakery stocked, even though I was busy managing and preparing orders at the counter. A guest even made my day when he told me that I have a beautiful smile while I was at the cash register.

During this first week on my own, my manager pulled me aside into her office and gave my assessment to officially "earn my ears" after training. Every role has an assessment after training, but each location and role does it differently. Some of my roommates had to do theirs on a computer in the form of a multiple-choice test, but mine was rather straightforward and easy. My manager simply had me sign a few papers to complete my training folder, and then asked me a few questions such as, "What's in our Polynesian salad?" and "What time do we change from breakfast to lunch?" After asking a handful of these types of questions, she asked whether I needed any clarification about anything that might not have been fully explained to me during my training. I couldn't think of anything at the time, which meant I was completely finished and had officially earned my ears!

Along with adjusting and becoming more comfortable with all the various roles in my restaurant, I was starting to get to know my coworkers as well. It was neat working with other college program students from around the country and learning about their reasons for participating in the program. Some of them were attending school in Louisiana, Alabama, and Virginia. Later, an international student from Brazil joined our little ohana at Capt. Cook's. I was also slowly getting to know the culinary team since I was behind the counter so often. Everyone was really nice, which helped me feel more at ease at my job. Coworkers definitely can make or break your experience at your location, and I was thankful that I had a good group of people during my program.

CHAPTER SIXTEEN

Meeting Fellow Vloggers

More college program cast members arrived as the weeks went by, including many of the friends I made through Facebook, YouTube, and Tumblr. I was excited to finally meet Meriem, Christine, and Mitch and Trey. Meriem surprised me at work the first time I met her. She was buying Dole Whip with a friend and planned on watching the fireworks on the beach. Our conversation was brief, but we'd be able to spend plenty of time together over the next few months.

Mitch, my fellow YouTube video blogger, arrived a few weeks after me. When he had finished Traditions, we chose a day that we both had off from work to meet in Hollywood Studios and film a video together. Our vlogging partners (Sara and Trey) were both unavailable because of work, but a couple other cast members from YouTube were going to meet up with us at Magic Kingdom later to film one large collaboration video.

Mitch and I met in the early afternoon after he finished his first day of orientation at Hollywood Studios in attractions. I had thought he would just change backstage and meet me after his shift, but by the time I arrived at the park, he was heading back to his apartment. Needless to say, I had a lot of free time to kill while I waited for him to return.

One newfound hobby I took up in the park was people watching. Going to the parks as a cast member and as a general guest are two completely different experiences. It's interesting to observe tourists and guests walking around the park enjoying their vacation in various ways. There's always the family scrutinizing the park map with furrowed brows while trying to decide which attraction to conquer next. Occasionally, you'll see a horde of individuals collectively chanting, all wearing the same light blue shirt while following a tour guide's flag. A tiny princess will squeal with glee as she snatches her first Disney churro from her dad's hands, her hair glittering with pixie dust and her dress matching that of her favorite princess. It was fascinating to think that each of these families, friends, and groups had their own stories, and each of those stories collided in this specific Disney park at the same exact moment.

Two street performances that I had never watched all the way through would arrive every few hours in front of the Sorcerer's Hat. Mulch, Sweat, and Shears paraded to their stage area with their beat-up yellow pick up truck and trailer covered in shrubbery and instruments. This rugged group of men rock out to classic tunes such as "Life in the Fast Lane" by the Eagles and "Free Ride" by The Edgar Winter Group. I wasn't too familiar with this kind of music, but the band was interactive with the guests and even invited some of them to play along with the cowbell.

The other performance in front of the Sorcerer's Hat was called Disney Channel Rocks. This show was a little more up my alley because I had absolutely adored Disney Channel through middle school and high school. I used to have a *High School Musical* poster in my room, and I was determined that Joe Jonas from the Jonas Brothers was going to be my future husband. Disney Channel Rocks brought back my childhood with their performances of songs from *The Cheetah Girls*, *Camp Rock*, and of course, *High School Musical*. They encouraged everyone to dance and sing along. I wished that I were younger, because I knew the words to the songs and the dance moves more than the children in the audience at the time (which was rather sad). Unfortunately, Disney Channel Rocks was discontinued a few months later.

I checked in with Mitch after watching the shows and observing guests, only to learn that he had just gotten back on the bus and was on his way. The bus to Hollywood Studios seemed to take forever, so I needed to find something else to pass a good chunk of my time alone in the park.

While walking away from the Sorcerer's Hat I noticed an exhibit I had never seen before called Walt Disney: One Man's Dream. It was a walk-through gallery about seminal moments in Walt Disney's life, starting from his youth in small-town Marceline, Missouri, all the way to his dreams and plans for his project in Florida, which he envisioned as EPCOT, a working "city of tomorrow", but which became, after his death, the Walt Disney World theme park. Casually strolling through the exhibit and seeing all of the concept art from Walt's early movies, as well as snippets of video here and there to coincide with some of the historic props, made me swell with pride and emotion. It was hard to believe that this man started from nothing and pursued his dreams and changed the world. Without Walt, I wouldn't have had the opportunity to work in such a magical place, wouldn't have met so many new friends, and wouldn't have had this incredible adventure. Families wouldn't have unforgettable memories of time spent together in the parks, and so many movies would never have touched the hearts of children and adults across the globe.

A quick beep and vibrate from my phone interrupted my thoughts. Mitch had finally made it to the park, so I scurried to meet him at the entrance. As soon as we saw each other, we hugged and agreed to ride Rock 'n' Roller Coaster first. We walked down Sunset Boulevard while he told me about his day and apologized for taking so long to meet with me. He said he was going to be an usher at Fantasmic!, which was slightly disappointing for him because he had hoped to be assigned to an actual ride, not a show. Mitch's ultimate dream was to become an Imagineer and design rides for Disney, so he wanted to learn all there was to know about a ride, any ride, during his internship. This is just another example of why you can't have any expectations or assumptions on where you will be placed for the Disney College Program. (Mitch eventually was able to cross-train at Rock 'n' Roller Coaster and loved working both locations for the rest of his program.)

We started our first collaboration video blog while waiting in line for Rock 'n' Roller Coaster, simply explaining what we were doing and why our video partners weren't with us. Soon after, we learned that two other YouTube vloggers wanted to meet and hang at one of the parks, so at the last minute we decided to meet them in Magic Kingdom after one of them was finished her afternoon Traditions class.

Mitch knew these two other people; I didn't. I hadn't watched either of their YouTube channels before I started my program, which is something I remedied after meeting them in person. Raisa had completed an entire Disney College Program in California before moving to Florida and participating here. She used to be a PhotoPass photographer in Disneyland, but now she was going to be a character attendant in Magic Kingdom. It was her first time in Florida, and I was excited to meet someone else who knew Disneyland better than Disney World. The other vlogger has been working in Florida for a long time and has a popular YouTube Channel called Ryan O's Disney Show.

The four of us introduced ourselves and made a beeline to Space Mountain. I was thrilled to hear that Raisa shared my same dislike for this version of Space Mountain compared to the one in Disneyland after riding it for her first time. After exploring Tomorrowland for a bit and filming some video for Mitch's channel, we continued to stroll our way to the new Storybook Circus to ride Dumbo, then found ourselves on the Winnie the Pooh attraction near Fantasyland. We ended our night on a relaxed note, and before we knew it, Magic Kingdom was going to close. We filmed one last goodbye scene while walking down Main Street, promising we'd continue to have collaboration videos in the future during our programs. (Unfortunately, this didn't often happen, although I did make a couple of guest appearances in Raisa's and Mitch's videos over the next few months.)

Meeting fellow YouTube video bloggers increased my excitement to meet more of the friends I had made online, but first they needed to arrive in Florida and join the Disney family.

CHAPTER SEVENTEEN

Animals and Norway

Sara and I had a mutual day off a few weeks after training, and Lizzie had a shift late in the day, so the three of us decided it was the perfect opportunity to explore Animal Kingdom and Epcot together. We rocked out to One Direction as we attempted to find our way to Animal Kingdom, and after getting lost a couple times we arrived in the nearly empty parking lot, which was nice to see. We entered the park and jetted our way to Africa to visit our roommate Sarah at Kilimanjaro Safaris. We were thrilled to hear that she was currently giving tours and hopped in the front row of her massive safari truck to surprise her when she pulled up to the loading dock. I had my phone out ready to videotape her entire tour.

Once her truck was loaded and ready to go, we took off on our two-week trek through the Harambe Wildlife Reserve to explore and observe many different kinds of exotic animals.

"Over here on the right is the okapi. The okapi has striped legs kind of like a zebra, but it's actually the only known relative of the giraffe."

As soon as Sarah started to say her first fact, we tried to contain our laughter because this was the part of her spiel that she continuously recited to us back at the apartment. To this day, I will probably never forget what the okapi is and that it's the only known relative to the giraffe.

"And right here there is a giant bird, that is called a Saddle-billed stork..."

We continued our way through the various landscapes and witnessed a tower of giraffes enjoying some shade underneath tall trees, a few lions sprawled upon massive rocks, as well as a massive group of Nile crocodiles together basking in the sunshine. It was a special treat to have the ability to see these animals up close and personal. It must be an incredible experience for Sarah to be able to "visit" these beautiful creatures many times per day as part of her job.

The tour came an end and we bid Sarah goodbye. As we exited the attraction, we found ourselves at the Pangani Forest Exploration Trail, a tropical forest exhibit that includes unusual birds, hippos, gorillas, and various other animals. Of course, as we made our way into the first part of the exhibit, Sara was more interested in the adorable standard duck instead of the exotic fish surrounding us in crystal clear tanks. (Although I have to admit, the duck *was* cute.)

After the fish, we explored farther down the trail and into a large hut. Inside, we noticed a handful of gorillas enjoying their afternoon on the grass. I was surprised to see a baby gorilla sporadically running around in bursts of energy as its mother tried her best to keep him nearby. On the other side of the hut we noticed some meerkats; adult guests would point them out to their children and say, "Look honey! It's Timon, from *The Lion King!*"

We continued through the exhibit to another hut, which contained rather random animals such as turtles and naked mole rats. We didn't spend too much time in this area except to cheer on a speedy turtle traveling down a few of his rocks in his little tank. Once he made it to the bottom, we headed out in pursuit for somewhere to eat lunch.

Pizzafari was calling our name, and the three of us enjoyed delicious Italian sandwiches, pizza, and chips. Lizzie had to leave for work, so after we finished eating we parted ways and Sara and I journeyed straight to Asia to ride Expedition Everest for an hour until the park closed. This was one of my favorite attractions, and it became Sara's newly found all-time favorite ride.

The week after our Animal Kingdom adventure, I finally met Christine in person. She had just finished training and joined Lizzie and me to venture and explore Epcot together. In addition to hanging out with Christine in Epcot, I had my heart set on some orange chicken in the Chinese Pavilion of the World Showcase.

The three of us chatted and laughed over our Chinese food and discovered something quite incredible. Lizzie and Christine both lived in Long Island, but what we soon found out was that before the college program, they both had worked in the same shopping mall and lived relatively close to each other. It's crazy to think that out of everywhere in Long Island, I managed to introduce two people to each other who might have casually interacted at their previous jobs.

We finished lunch and strolled around the World Showcase, just taking in its breathtaking beauty. Just the fact that you can be in

China one moment and then find yourself in Germany, Morocco, or the United Kingdom in a matter of steps is something you can't do anywhere else. This was my first time exploring the different pavilions. The only pavilions I remembered from my family trip to Walt Disney World were Mexico and Japan; all the others were new to me.

While exploring, we stopped and took photos with Duffy the Disney bear. I've never really understood where Duffy came from besides that he was Mickey's teddy bear, but he was adorable and extremely soft to hug. There was also barely any line to meet him, which is always a plus.

One pavilion I didn't even know existed was the one dedicated to Norway. I found it somewhat random that they even had a Norway pavilion, but I was even more surprised when the girls told me there was a ride there. Sure enough, if you look closely you can see Viking-style boats turning a corner in an open window in the main building. Liz told me it was similar to Splash Mountain, just with a smaller drop. I was all for trying it at least once, but little did I know what I was going to experience.

Inside the queue, a huge mural dominated the entire wall in the loading dock, filled with muscular and bearded Norwegian men working on oil rigs, climbing mountains, and sailing ships. The three of us settled into our own miniature Viking longboat and sailed into darkness.

For a few moments, it was pitch black with winds howling in the distance. Suddenly, a bright light shined in front of us, with a commanding voice booming overhead: "Those who seek the spirit of Norway, face peril and adventure..."

I found everything about this ride to be creepy. I don't seek the spirit of Norway! What's even going on?

Lizzie and Christine started cackling over my commentary, even though I was legitimately confused and freaked out. The darkness continued along with the god-like narrator, leading us to a group of Vikings on ships interacting with each other (attempting to barter and trade, I assumed).

We continued to the next room. "There are those who seek the spirit of Norway...where trolls still prowl the water's edge."

What?! Trolls? I don't want anything to do with trolls! This ride was so incredibly uncomfortable and we weren't even halfway finished.

We crept through more darkness and silence before massive glaring eyes appeared out of nowhere and an ugly, three-headed, bearded creature chanted, "HALT! This is troll country! You will disappear! DISAPPEAR! DISAPPEAR!"

The next thing we knew our Viking ship was slowly reversing its direction, and then suddenly propelling us toward...polar bears? One colossal polar bear stood on its hind legs and roared.

How did we go from the forest to polar bears? This isn't making any sense. My friends were still thoroughly amused over my distress with this attraction and continued to laugh.

Our ship continued to travel in reverse toward an opening to the outside world. As the back of our boat peeked out through the window, part of me was secretly hoping we would just fall out of the pavilion. It'd be an ugly fall, but it would mean I'd finally be done with this ride.

Unfortunately, my wish didn't come true, because more trolls peeked over the bushes as we moved forward, cackling over our imminent doom. Before we could even think twice about what was happening, we plummeted down a 28-foot drop into a stormy North Sea. Thunder clapped and lightning flashed above the choppy waves. We were steered around various oilrigs scattered across the water. We only had a few moments to try and comprehend what we were experiencing before our ship came to an abrupt stop.

The god-like voice boomed one last time: "Norway's spirit will always be adventure."

And my adventure will always be avoiding this ride. I jetted out of the ship as soon as we arrived at the unload dock. The three of us raced past the theater where guests had the option to watch a six-minute video about tourism in Norway, and then dodged all the vendors in the Norwegian gift shop. Finally, we were free.

I still don't understand why anyone actually enjoyed that attraction. Needless to say, I avoided Maelstrom at all costs for the rest of my program. It's now gone, soon to be replaced with something from *Frozen*. I wonder what they're going to do with that polar bear.

CHAPTER EIGHTEEN

An Eventful Nine Days

As I entered the second month of my program, I was growing more accustomed to the routine of working five days a week. Usually, my days off were Sundays and Mondays, but this changed one week because I requested Valentine's Day and my birthday off (my birthday is the day after Valentine's). These days happened to fall on a Thursday and a Friday, which squished my two work weeks into one long chain. This particular stretch of shifts spanned a total of nine days in a row— definitely a challenge to endure at some points.

After the first three or four days, I started developing the habit of simply waking up, getting dressed in my costume, walking to the bus stop, and heading to my shift without thinking twice about it. I was now much more comfortable with every position, and I even knew how to explain the dining plan without having to think twice about it.

Since I was growing more comfortable at work, I was able to feel more at ease when interacting with guests. The easiest place to do this was at the cash register, since the check out and payment process was one big series of guest interactions. Many guests started asking where I was from, since those participating in the college program have their college names printed on their nametag instead of their home towns. Most guests who asked me didn't know much about California besides Hollywood and San Francisco. However, I did meet one man who grew up in the same city as my mom, and even knew about my city! We talked about its well-known restaurants, the college, and other aspects of my little town. I was impressed.

On my sixth day of work in a row, I had my first morning shift at 7:00 AM. I hadn't had a morning shift since training, so I was nervous. I was more familiar with the lunch/dinner menu, not the breakfast menu. My fingers were crossed that my managers would place me in the dining room that day, since I would be able to avoid my lack of breakfast menu knowledge in that position. Of course, they put me on the cast register that day…the position where you needed to know everything about the menu and the breakfast portion of the dining plan, which is a little different than lunch and dinner. When I told my manager that I was rusty at this position for morning shifts, she was helpful and reminded me about everything I needed to know. I learned that breakfast on the cash register was much easier than the afternoon, since the dining plan for breakfast required only a drink and an entrée (as opposed to a drink, entrée, and dessert for lunch and dinner). The guests had a much simpler time understanding the process in the morning, which also made my job easier.

I grew more comfortable at cashier during this shift, even though it can be one of the more stressful positions when Capt. Cook's gets busy. Our system for the cash register isn't the most efficient, but if both you and the other cashier know how to handle the flow of guests, you'll be able to work through the crowd quickly. The cash registers are stationed in the middle of the restaurant with the lines forming on both sides, and we alternate sides after each transaction. Sometimes guests can get frustrated when they'll be next in line for me on one side, but I'd have to take someone farther back on the other side to ensure that both lines flow consistently.

During this particular morning shift, I completed a transaction with a guest on my left and then waved to help the next person on my right side. The woman on my right offered for the man on my left to go first because he was waiting longer than her.

As soon as she offered, the man rolled his eyes and said: "No, let her go. She's been whining enough about waiting anyway."

The woman looked aghast and offended, and the next thing I knew her husband appeared on my left and began staring the man down.

"What did you just say to my wife? Where are you from?"

The woman piped in, "Obviously not from the South."

"Boston? New York?" Her husband continued. "You're a Yankees fan, aren't you?"

I could feel the tension brewing between the three guests, and I had a feeling the situation wasn't going to improve.

"Call security." The non-Southern guest turned toward me. "Call security."

My heart was in my throat. The man wouldn't respond to anything the husband and wife were trying to tell him, and the couple continued to verbally attack him, trying to raise some sort of reaction.

I picked up the phone and tried to find the number for security, but there wasn't one on the list at the register. My coworker on the register in front of me called our manager, and I was able to calm the guests down and continue with the line before anything serious happened. My manager arrived a few minutes later and talked to the Southern couple and handled the rest of the conflict.

I tried to focus on each guest interaction for the next hour to try and distract myself from what had just happened. I was a little shaken up from the experience. I was literally in between two guests arguing with each other and almost starting a fight. Thankfully, this was the only time I had to encounter such a volatile situation during my program.

Later in the day, we had a slower flow of guests, which was nice after the big breakfast rush. As I was organizing my conglomeration of receipts, a little girl walked up to me and asked whether I remembered my customers.

I bent down to her level. "What's wrong, princess? Are you looking for someone?"

"Do you remember a woman named Julia?" she asked softly.

Something clicked in my mind as I realized this young girl couldn't find her mother. I asked if she was lost and she nodded her head slowly. I noticed her eyes were slightly red and swollen from crying, so I told my coworker the situation and had someone hop on my register while I walked with the girl to the front desk. Luckily, the girl had her mom's cell phone number memorized, so the coordinator at the front desk kept calling until the mom picked up. Her mom was on the patio of my restaurant, which was an area the little girl couldn't easily see. The coordinator told her mom that I would meet with her near the pool outside to ensure her daughter got back safely.

On the way to the pool, the young girl and I talked about how she and her family were at Disney for her cousin's cheerleading competition in Hollywood Studios.

"Where are you from?" she asked me as we passed the massive fountain in the lobby.

"I'm from California!"

Her brow furrowed. "Why aren't you living in California right now?"

"Well, I came here to work for Disney!" I replied matter-of-factly.

"Since you work here, can you go to the parks whenever you want?" She grew excited.

"Yup! Whenever I'm not working!" I responded as we approached my restaurant.

"Wow, I'm jealous."

We walked through Capt. Cook's and out the back toward the pool. As soon as we walked down the stairs I found her mom waving and running to hug her daughter. She thanked me profusely and I left as soon as I knew the situation was safe. I returned to my cash register, told my coworkers that we had found the girl's mom, and breathed a sigh of relief. My first morning shift was certainly turning into an eventful day.

On another day during the seemingly never-ending stretch of shifts, I was in the dining room bussing tables. It was a slow afternoon, so when I finished wiping off all of the tables I walked over to my coworker at the cash register to see how she was doing. I looked down behind the computer screen and noticed some small white squares tucked behind some chords. I reached my hand to the back of the register and found out that I had discovered some long-lost Mickey stickers. For some reason during the beginning of my program, Mickey stickers were difficult to find. Some other locations, such as the restaurant where Sara worked, always had an over-abundance of stickers and Mickey straws to give to guests to make small but memorable magical moments.

Some of my coworkers who had been at Cook's for a long time told me that my restaurant used to make magical moments by giving out small cupcakes with lit candles for guests' birthdays. Once our menu switched to gourmet cupcakes, they were too expensive to give out to guests for free anymore. This was disappointing to hear, but I was excited to have discovered the stickers behind the cash register that day. I immediately put them in the pockets of my apron and scouted out possible moments to give them to guests.

Later during this shift, a little boy with two older siblings (all very young) walked in with their parents. The parents had a balloon, and everyone had an "I'm Celebrating" button to compliment the little boy's birthday pin on his shirt. I waited for the perfect moment, and while the little boy was standing on his own near the cooler, I knelt down to his level.

"Is it your birthday?" I asked him excitedly.

The boy stood there and stared at me, wide eyed and in silence. I asked again gently, trying not to scare him.

When he still didn't answer, his dad saw me and stepped forward, "Yes, it's his birthday."

I pulled out a sticker, "Mickey told me it was your birthday today, and he wanted me to give you this special sticker! Would you like to have it?"

He stared, completely frozen. I'm pretty sure I scared the poor boy half to death. I turned to his siblings and offered them stickers, too, which they excitedly accepted. I gave the birthday boy's sticker to his father, who was gracious throughout. Even though the boy was a little shy, I still felt giddy and excited over my first magical moment. Going that extra mile is a rewarding feeling that can't be compared to anything else.

The rest of the week consisted of me trying to stay awake enough to survive the long nine days in a row. Guests began to recognize me after a few days, sometimes asking if I ever went home. One woman even asked me if I was an animated character, because it seemed like I was always on the go and constantly working.

Just when I thought the shifts would never end, my ninth day finally arrived. As soon as the clock said 3:30, I whipped off my gloves, threw my spray bottle in the stock closet, snatched my purse from my locker, ran to the bus, threw open my apartment door, and crashed on my bed. Nothing felt as amazing as finally lying down while knowing I didn't have to go to work for the next two days. Even though I wasn't working, this was the only afternoon I had to relax, because the next two days were filled with nonstop plans in the parks.

But first, it was time for a long-awaited nap.

CHAPTER NINETEEN

A Magical Birthday

My grandparents visited on Valentine's Day. It was their first time experiencing Animal Kingdom and Hollywood Studios, so I was excited to show them around. I woke up early to catch the bus and meet them shortly after park opening, but they were stuck in traffic and said they would arrive at Animal Kingdom a little later than expected. I took this opportunity to walk around the park and indulge in the simple pleasures of people watching, much like when I was waiting for Mitch in Hollywood Studios.

Animal Kingdom was rather empty since it was still very close to opening, but while I was walking around I grew wary of the dark grey clouds looming over the park. I knew Florida was known for its frequent rain, but it had been extremely dry for the month and a half leading up to Valentine's Day. Of course, a few minutes after strolling around the park on my own, it started to sprinkle on the only day my grandparents came to visit from California. I hid in a little cave off of the walkway, where a young girl and her mother were also seeking refuge. A PhotoPass photographer was protecting his camera equipment and whistling a happy tune. The little girl danced along to his whistling as I sat off to the side enjoying the pleasant scene.

My phone rang after a few minutes with my grandma on the other line. They had already parked and were walking through the security tents. By then, the rain had subsided and so I was able to walk back to the entrance without getting wet. I found my grandparents as I exited the park and ran to give them a huge hug. I was so excited to show them around these two parks for their first time, as well as tell them all about the experience I was having so far in Florida.

Our main priority was to ride Expedition Everest, which both of my grandparents enjoyed. On our way to the attraction, it started raining again. My grandpa decided to purchase one of the infamous Disney ponchos to keep him dry, which I found hilarious. You can always spot the tourists when you notice large groups or families huddled together in the highlighter yellow ponchos with the "Disney Parks" logo slapped on the back.

We chose to get FastPasses for Everest since the line was a little too long for comfort, and then hopped next door to watch the Flights of Wonder bird show. The birds were spectacular, and we enjoyed the performance. The rest of the day we rode DINOSAUR, returned for Everest, ate lunch at Yak and Yeti, took photos in front of the Tree of Life, and adventured on the Kilimanjaro Safaris. The rain was starting to get worse, so we decided to head to Hollywood Studios for the rest of the day.

By the time we made it to the other park, the rain had turned into a downpour. For weeks it hadn't done more than sprinkle, and now it had to pour when my grandparents were here. In addition to the rain, all of the rides in Studios seemed to be ridiculously busy. Both Tower of Terror and Rock 'n' Roller Coaster had lines that lasted for over an hour. Our first priority was to find somewhere dry, which led us to the Great Movie Ride, the Walt Disney: One Man's Dream exhibit, and dinner at Sci-Fi Dine-In Theater. The old-fashioned drive-in theater theme is a neat experience, and my club sandwich with sweet potato fries was delicious.

After dinner, we called it a night. We drove back to my apartment, said our goodbyes, and I crashed on the couch with Liz and Sara. The two of them were discussing whether to attend the face character audition scheduled for the next morning, which was also the same day as the events planned for my birthday. Right before we went to sleep, we decided it'd be a fun and different experience to just auditions a try and see what might happen. Sarah and Carmen were also planning on auditioning, so we woke up at the crack of dawn to start my birthday off with an audition to join Disney's entertainment department.

I had lunch reservations at noon for all of us at 50's Prime Time Café in Hollywood Studios, which we were certain we would make if the auditions started around eight in the morning. However, we were off to a late start and arrived to see that there were over 700 people at the same audition. The line was out the door and down the sidewalk in the parking lot just to check in, and barely moving every few minutes. Bethany said she would meet us at the restaurant, just in case we took longer than we planned.

We slowly made our way into the building and finally checked in a couple hours later. After a cast member measured us to see how tall we were, we were assigned a number and asked to sit and wait in a giant room filled with other girls waiting to audition. To pass the time, my friends and I would point out specific girls to see which character or princess they most resembled.

We waited for at least another hour before our numbers were called, and I was growing a little worried about our lunch reservation. Bethany called and told us she couldn't accept our table until we had everyone in our party, and it didn't look like our group was going to be called to audition any time soon. I told Bethany to hang tight and that we were going to go straight to Hollywood Studios as quickly as possible when we were finished. Meriem was on her way to meet with Bethany, so everyone left for lunch was waiting at the audition.

Finally, after what seemed like forever, our group was called. We stood in numerical order according to the numbers on our nametags and marched in a single file line into the audition room.

The woman in charge of the audition stood front and center of the room and said: "Since this is a look-a-like audition, we are not going to ask you to do a dance number for us. All we'll be doing is play some music, walk around, and examine your faces. This may feel a little awkward! After we look at everyone, we'll immediately tell you if any of you are moving to the next round. Alright, everyone smile!"

Music started to play as the woman walked back and forth, staring directly at each and every one of us. All of us in the front row giggled nervously through the beginning of the process, but then she asked for us to move to the back of the room and for the line behind us to step forward. We went through this cycle until all of the rows of girls were reviewed. Finally, it was time for the results.

The casting woman returned to the front of the room, "Thank you girls for your time, but we will not be accepting any of you today."

I sighed and shrugged my shoulders. I wasn't very disappointed; I knew I wasn't going to be chosen. At least I had gone through the experience and given it a shot. What I was really concerned about, though, were the lunch reservations.

I looked at my watch: 12:30 pm. We were already late.

The four of us raced to Liz's car while I called Bethany. Meriem was already there with her, and we told them to inform the host or hostess at the restaurant that we'd arrive as soon as possible. I was ridiculously excited to eat at 50's Prime Time Café for the first time. This restaurant is designed to model off of a traditional kitchen and dining room from the 1950s. Their waiters and waitresses have a reputation for playing true to the time period, adapting the character of the traditional 1950s mother or father. One of my coworkers mentioned that the waiter in charge of her and her boyfriend's table actually gave my coworker's boyfriend a bib and spoon-fed his vegetables when he didn't finish his collard greens. Another time, one of my friends was caught uploading a picture on Instagram, which caused her waitress to send her to the corner of the room with her nose to the wall to make her think about proper manners at the dinner table. With all of these amazing stories in mind, I was curious to see what kind of experience we were going to have during our meal.

We finally arrived at Hollywood Studios and rushed to the restaurant about an hour after our scheduled reservation time. I walked up to the podium to check in with my tail between my legs, embarrassed about arriving so late. The hostess told us to wait a few minutes in the lounge area, and I breathed a sigh of relief that we were still going to be able to have our lunch. We had less people than I originally expected, due to work conflicts and simple exhaustion from waking up so early for auditions, which probably helped our situation when trying to get a table so long after our scheduled time.

While we were sitting in the lounge area, I thought it would be appropriate to start filming my birthday for a future YouTube video. I started scanning the room from my left, and as I slowly turned to my right I noticed a man in a bright blue and yellow shirt *glaring* at me.

"Are you Sara?" he questioned in a critical tone, eyebrows furrowed.

"Oh, hi, yes that's me..." I replied sheepishly.

He uncrossed his arms, waving a stack of menus in the air, "YOU MADE YOUR FRIENDS WAIT AN HOUR FOR YOU, AND YOU FINALLY SHOW UP AND ALL YOU HAVE TO SAY IS 'OH, HI'??"

I felt myself blush as I looked down and away from the host, ashamed of the situation, "I'm sorry! I didn't mean for this to happen!"

"Uh huh, sure," he turned on his heel and briskly walked away. "Follow me."

As we walked through the restaurant, I fell in love with the themed architecture and design. Little black-and-white televisions were stationed next to each dining room table, and old photos in clunky frames hung on the walls. Each family looked like they were at their own little dining room straight out of the 1950s; even the waiters and waitresses were wearing aprons, dresses, and suits to match the era.

Shortly after the host seated us at our table, our waitress arrived and gave us our silverware, all wrapped in napkins and in a pile.

"Hello, sweet things, I'm Aunt Annie and I'll be serving your meal today. I'll be right back, but when I return you better have set the table by then, you hear?" She pointed to the utensils and walked away. I was excited to see if anything funny or unique happened with our waitress later during our meal, but I was disappointed when the most interesting event was when we discovered that she was from the same hometown as Liz.

I ordered a heaping plate of fried chicken with collard greens. Bethany was the only one able to actually finish her entire meal, to which our waitress rewarded her with the "Clean Plate Award" and gave her a sticker. Sara ordered a huge helping of s'mores for dessert, but she and Carmen had to leave shortly afterward for work. The rest of us thanked our waitress, paid our tab, and made a beeline to Rock 'n' Roller Coaster for a quick ride before heading to Magic Kingdom.

During my college program, Disney's newest slogan and special plan for the year was called Limited Time Magic. This meant that each week or month, Disney had something special in store for its guests at the various parks. Since it was Valentine's Day week during my birthday, Disney's Limited Time Magic for the romantic holiday was called True Love Week, which allowed guests to meet the princesses with their designated prince. This was extremely rare; you hardly ever had the opportunity to meet both Rapunzel and Flynn Rider or Cinderella and Prince Charming together in Magic Kingdom. Since it was such a rare moment, I decided to go character hunting for the first time and meet all of the royal couples for the rest of the night.

We began our hunt in Town Square, where we would be able to meet Rapunzel, Aurora, and Cinderella with their true loves. The line was pretty lengthy, but this was expected since it was a special event. I was excited to meet Flynn Rider from *Tangled*; he was without a doubt my favorite Disney prince (next to Naveen from *The Princess and the Frog*). I found him hilarious and definitely easy on the eyes, which is strange to say about an animated character.

We met Rapunzel and Flynn first. I skipped forward when the character attendant gave the okay, and Rapunzel was ecstatic when she saw my birthday pin. Flynn reminded me that birthdays are her favorite things, which was proven when she started talking to me.

"It's your birthday? That's so exciting! You wanna know the best thing about birthdays? They come year after year after year after year…" she continued, jumping out of her skin. "Except if you're Mother Gothel, then you don't like birthdays at all."

"But then we'd push you out of the tower! And we wouldn't want that," Flynn chimed in.

"Ah, well, I'm not evil, so you don't have to worry about that," I responded right before we took a photo together.

Up next were Aurora and Prince Philip. Philip didn't say much, but Aurora asked about my day and whether I was enjoying my birthday. She also said that Merryweather would love my shirt, since blue is her favorite color. I asked Aurora about whether she preferred her dress in pink or blue, and she smiled and said: "I love them both equally, but since it's true love week I decided pink would fit the occasion."

The last royal couple in Town Square Theater was Cinderella and Prince Charming. Charming had a very deep voice, which I found kind of creepy. He and Cindy had little to say, except that they hoped all of my birthday wishes came true. After we took our photos together, we made our way down Main Street to meet one of my favorite Disney couples, Tiana and Naveen from *The Princess and the Frog*.

When it was my turn in line, I walked up and the two of them wished me a happy birthday and each gave me a hug. Naveen looked closely at me and questioned, "Have you met with us before?"

I grew confused, "No…this is my first time meeting you two."

"Hmm, that's interesting, because you look very familiar." He turned to Tiana, who shrugged her shoulders, clearly as lost as me.

"I do work here, though," I continued. "Maybe you've seen me around?"

When I told them I worked in foods in the Polynesian, Tiana chimed in, "Oh! What's your favorite seafood recipe at your restaurant?"

I froze. Even though I had been working in my resort for over a month, at that moment I couldn't think of a single item on our menu. I blurted, "Shrimp…shrimp sushi?"

While Tiana started to laugh, Naveen perked up: "Wait, you sell Dole Whip, don't you?"

My mouth dropped. "Yes, yes I do."

Later that night I discovered that Naveen remembered me from serving him Dole Whip within the past month. I unknowingly sold Dole Whip to Naveen. Disney truly is a small, small world.

We said goodbye to the wonderful couple and walked back down Main Street to watch the Electrical Parade. I was jumping out of my skin when the Donkey boy on the Pinocchio float actually shouted, "Happy birthday!" while waving to everyone in the crowd.

When the parade finished, we were about ready to call it a night. However, Meriem's roommate found us as we were on our way out and mentioned that she wanted to quickly see Snow White. I made a little squeal and my friends immediately knew we needed to meet Snow and her prince before we left. To add to the little surprise, Dopey was meeting guests with the couple!

Snow White has a special place in my heart. When I was very young, I would carry a Snow White doll with me everywhere I went, and my parents said I used to call her "No Night" when I was first learning to talk. On my birthday, I was wearing my favorite brand-new Snow White shirt, along with a bow I used for my Snow White costume that I had I pulled together for Halloween the previous year.

When Dopey saw my shirt, he clapped his hands and giddily skipped towards me, pulling me toward Snow and the Prince and pointing at my shirt. Snow smiled, "Yes, Dopey, that's me on her shirt!"

Snow continued to ask me about my birthday, and then asked whether I had my own prince or true love. When I responded no, Dopey jumped up and started pointing at himself. Snow reminded him that he already asked Meriem's roommate to be his true love, and then leaned in close to me to whisper, "Well, let me give you some advice. I found my true love by a wishing well. Maybe if you start spending some time near a wishing well you'll find a prince for yourself! Then he can pick you beautiful flowers, just like the ones behind us!" She motioned to the arrangement on the wall. "Dopey picked these, aren't they lovely?"

I nodded in agreement and the four of us posed for one last photo for the night. I thanked them as the next guests took their turn for their meet-and-greet session, and my group of friends decided it was finally time to end the night. While many of the girls went to find the bus to go home, Meriem and I hopped on the monorail to make one last stop.

Our monorail pulled up to the Polynesian and we walked down the stairs to Capt. Cook's. By the time we arrived, the main grill was closed and the graveyard cast member was preparing for the rest of the night. I found one of my managers helping around the restaurant and gently reminded her that it was my birthday. A few weeks ago, one of my coworkers visited the restaurant on her birthday, and my manager said that I was allowed a free Dole Whip if I came to see her on mine.

As promised, she saw my birthday pin and wished me a happy birthday as she gave me my free Dole Whip cup. I gave her a hug and filled my cup as high as I possible, creating what looked like the Leaning Tower of Dole Whip. Meriem thought I was crazy for serving myself so much, but I had to take advantage of the moment. It's not every day we got to have Dole Whip for free!

Overall, it was one of the best birthdays I've ever experienced. I've always dreamed of spending a birthday in Disney, and to be surrounded by amazing new friends is something I'll cherish.

CHAPTER TWENTY

A Grand Deployment

One aspect of the college program I had read about in blogs was deployment. Not every role participates in deployment. From what I witnessed during my program, it seemed like quick service food and beverage and merchandise were the main roles that had college program interns deployed.

If a cast member is deployed, it means they will temporarily work at a different location on Disney property. Many times this occurs during slow seasons to help you reach your required hours per week, or at a location that might be understaffed and need the extra cast members. During my program, many QSFB cast members were deployed to Epcot's Flower and Garden Festival, which meant others were deployed to fill their place in their home locations. Because of this, I wasn't too surprised when I discovered "Deployed—Gasparilla Grill" on my newest schedule one day. I learned that Gasparilla Grill was located in the Grand Floridian, Disney World's fanciest and most expensive resort.

One other girl from Capt. Cook's had been deployed there. She was on the same bus as me one night after a long 1:30 am shift, which is where I met her for the first time. I asked her about her experience at Gasparilla Grill (nicknamed Gaspy's) and she told me that she had enjoyed her time in the different location, and that it was nice to change the scenery a bit after constantly working at Cook's for such a long time.

I was 100% on my own for figuring out where to get my new costume, which bus to take, where to clock in, and who to ask for help with my job. It was a lot to absorb at first, but I started by taking a quick visit to Gaspy's for lunch with Liz one day before work.

It was a nice quick service restaurant. Absolutely everything was white, including the cast members' costumes. While I was paying for my chicken nuggets, I asked the cashier about where to find the entrance for backstage, as well as whether I should buy white shoes for the costume (my work shoes were black). She explained as best as she could where to walk from the bus stop, and she did suggest I find white shoes, since my black ones would clash with the restaurant's theme.

The weekend before my deployment I made a quick trip to the Florida Mall to purchase some cheap, white, non-slip shoes from Payless. In a stroke of luck, the Polynesian shared the same costuming center as the Grand Floridian, which made finding my costume relatively easy. The Grand was also on the same bus route as the Polynesian; the challenge was still finding the backstage entrance from the bus stop.

There were quite a few Grand cast members getting off at the same stop as me, so I simply followed a few housekeepers to find my way. When I entered the building, I found a girl in the Gasparilla costume and an "Earning My Ears" ribbon under her nametag. I told her I was from another resort and that this was my first day at the Grand. She directed me to the manager's office and told him about the situation. He seemed confused and didn't seem to be expecting me, but he helped me out and showed me around for a bit before putting me to work.

I started out at window, where I took orders from guests and then gave the person in charge of the fryer the order. It was rather simple, and if a guest ever had any questions about the menu, prices, or the dining plan related to this restaurant, I would turn to my left and ask the girl next to me for help. This was one aspect I wasn't too fond of during deployment. I was so comfortable with the menu and setup at Cook's that I could answer almost any question a guest threw at me. Since I was new at Gaspy's, I didn't know specifics about directions around the hotel for guests, or even what was on the menu.

My second day at Gaspy's I was runner/busser. As the runner, I was in charge of bringing the trays of food to the guests at their table, similar to a sit-down restaurant. I enjoyed this position. There was much more opportunity for guest interaction while bringing the trays to the tables. If I wasn't running an order to a table, I was greeting guests and asking if they needed any help.

On my third day, business was slow so I walked up to a family and asked if they had any questions about the menu. When the parents said they didn't need any help, I knelt down to their two daughters' level and was about to compliment them on their beautiful princess dresses. Before I could say anything, the oldest asked, "Are you a princess?"

I was flattered, especially since I was basically just wearing a white shirt, pants, apron, and hat. Nothing about it screamed "princess", but I played along.

"Well, my name actually means princess! Are you a princess?"

She nodded shyly and said yes. I asked her who her favorite princess was, and she began naming almost every princess. In the end, she told me there was no way she could choose, she loves all of them. It was adorable!

At the end of the week, I was mainly in charge of bussing. I helped the runner when the restaurant grew busy, but it never got too overwhelming. For about four days in a row, I had shifts that all ended at 1:30 in the morning, which made me exhausted by the end of my deployment. I started creating a fun little friendship with the graveyard cast member, since he knew I was new and never actually trained to work there. In fact, I developed quite a good group of friends while working at the Grand. Both my coworkers and managers helped me feel welcome and at home in the new location. It was bittersweet returning to the Polynesian the following week. I missed my Cook's coworkers, but I really enjoyed working in Gaspy's.

I would see my Gaspy coworkers every once in a while throughout the rest of my program. I remember some of them were trying to get their manager to make Disney deploy me again so I could work with them another week. I would've loved the opportunity, but it never happened. I kept telling them I'd try and pick up a shift, but because of my schedule that never happened, either. It was tough trying to pick up a shift when I was already scheduled five days a week.

I loved my experience at the Grand. One day while arriving on the bus, I saw a newlywed couple in Cinderella's carriage as part of one of Disney's fairytale weddings, which is something not everyone gets to see. I loved the pace of the restaurant, as well as the level of guest interaction. My coworkers and managers topped it off to create an overall great experience, and I really wish I had had the chance to work at Gaspy's one more time during my program.

CHAPTER TWENTY-ONE

A Trip to Hogwarts

Throughout the month of February, Sara had a nasty illness. I was impressed to see her fight her sickness and still maintain an amazing reputation at work. From what I was hearing, she was shining at the Wilderness Lodge. She loved her job, and everyone loved her. She would come home with stories about her manager giving her Four Keys Cards (rewards for doing a good job) and interactions with families staying at her resort.

Once she was better, we decided it was time for "Sara Squared" to journey to Hogwarts together. It would be her first time, and she absolutely loves Harry Potter. Liz, Sara and I met at Meriem's apartment for breakfast before we adventured to Universal. I was wearing my Iron Man/arc reactor shirt and Liz had her favorite Spiderman tee, so we were ready to fit in with the Marvel section of Islands of Adventure. Our main goals for the day were to show Sara around the Wizarding World of Harry Potter, drink endless amounts of Butterbeer, and meet Captain America. With delicious food in our bellies and passes in hand, we took the rare moment to journey outside of Disney property.

Sara was giddy with excitement the closer we approached Hogwarts. As soon as we stepped through the majestic archway into the Wizarding World, her eyes widened and her mouth dropped with disbelief. We were officially walking through Hogsmeade, a little village straight out of the world of Harry Potter.

As we walked past the snow-tipped shops and restaurants, we discovered that our friends Katie and Giselle, along with their roommate Ashley, were in the park as well. After meeting up with them, we marched straight to Harry Potter and the Forbidden Journey (the main attraction inside Hogwarts).

Even though I had visited Hogwarts and the Wizarding World a few years ago with my family during its opening summer, I was still in awe over the incredible detail Universal put into creating the attraction: the gorgeous statues, the endless moving portraits, the Gryffindor Common Room, Dumbledore's office, the greenhouse, and even the Defense Against the Dark Arts classroom. Everything felt as if you were stepping straight into the movie, which is an absolute dream for any Harry Potter fan.

While we were waiting in line, we overheard an interesting conversation between two guests. We couldn't hear everything, but we could distinctly hear one of them say, "Did you know this is the biggest and most expensive attraction that Disney has ever invested in?"

We had to hold back our laughter. This woman thought they were in a Disney park...or at least that Disney had an affiliation with Universal Studios and Harry Potter. Sure, they're both major entertainment resorts, but they're very different in many ways. You'd think people would know when they're not on Disney property, but you'd be surprised with how many we'd see wearing Mickey ears and Disney birthday buttons around Universal.

After braving a dragon, Dementors, and the Whomping Willow on the attraction inside Hogwarts, we rode the dueling roller coaster Dragon Challenge before eating lunch in the Three Broomsticks. I had chicken salad, while some of the others had potpie and pea soup. We had to have Butterbeer with our meal, which can be described perfectly with Sara's first sentence after trying it for the first time: "Oh my gosh, that's heavenly." I have yet to find any drink similar to Butterbeer. It's a unique mix of butterscotch and cream soda. No trip to Wizarding World is complete without at least one Butterbeer.

We finished our meals and strolled through the shops around Hogsmeade. I ended up purchasing a bottle of Pumpkin Juice, and Sara resisted the temptation to buy an adorable Pygmy Puff (which is basically a cute little fluffy stuffed mouse). One attraction I had never experienced before was Ollivanders, where select guests can experience what it's like to choose their own wand. The line wasn't too bad when we were nearby, so we walked inside.

The walls of the shop were filled with dusty boxes of various wands. Mr. Ollivander emerged from behind a shelf, searching for his newest pupil. As soon as he settled on Katie, we squealed with joy. We had heard that most of the time Mr. Ollivander chooses younger children to join the experience, but this time he chose probably the biggest Harry Potter fan out of everyone there.

Katie skipped to the center of the room, and I immediately pulled out my camera to film the entire show. After a few mishaps with incompatible wands, Katie grabbed hold of her perfect choice, lights beaming from above and music singing from the heavens. When it was over, she bought her wand and has been happy with it ever since.

The rest of the day was spent riding roller coasters in the Marvel section of Islands of Adventure, meeting Captain America (who was somewhat disappointed to hear that Iron Man was my favorite superhero), and adventuring into the Universal Studios side of the park. It was ridiculously hot outside, but we were thankful that most of the attractions in Universal Studios were indoors.

We braved The Mummy more than once, battled each other's alien attacking skills in Men in Black, and tried our best to avoid motion sickness in the Simpsons virtual roller coaster. I even rode the E.T. attraction for the first time. I realize it's a classic, but it really freaked me out. I had never watched all of *E.T.*, so the experience was strange for me. I was pleasantly surprised to see a section of the park dedicated to *Fieval Goes West*, which was a movie I adored watching as a child. By the end of the day, we were all exhausted. It was nice to spend a day outside of Disney, and it was an even lovelier surprise to meet with Katie, Giselle, and Ashley.

I also traveled to Universal with some of my coworkers at Capt. Cook's later in my program, and even ended up seeing my favorite singer Demi Lovato in concert for free with Liz during Universal's Mardi Gras celebration. It was a great place to spend time with new friends whenever we wanted a little break from the hectic Disney cast member life.

CHAPTER TWENTY-TWO

Dapper Day

Twice a year, guests in both Disneyland and Disney World celebrate the unofficial Disney holiday, Dapper Day. Guests in the parks dress up in their Sunday best, most of the time inspired by fashion from the 1950s. Disneyland guests created this tradition to pay homage to the opening of the park in 1955, when everyone dressed in their most dapper outfits to spend the day in the Happiest Place on Earth.

I had seen pictures of previous Dapper Days in Disneyland, but never had the chance to officially attend one until my program. I was excited to dress all fancy and spend a day in the parks with Liz, Meriem, Raisa, and any other friends we happened to see along the way.

The three of us decided to create Disneybound Dapper Day outfits modeled on Disney characters. After many hours searching in the Florida mall, I was able to find an adorable black-and-white polka-dotted dress. When I added a solid blue necklace that I already owned, my outfit resembled that of Perdita from *101 Dalmations*. Liz discovered a beautiful light blue dress to resemble Wendy from one of her favorite movies, *Peter Pan*. Raisa had the a dress similar to Ariel's outfit during the "Kiss the Girl" segment in *The Little Mermaid*.

I had work in the afternoon on Dapper Day, but I was able to venture through Magic Kingdom beforehand and make it to the meet up in front of the castle, where everyone who was dressed in a Disneybound-inspired dapper outfit came together to take a group photo in front of Cinderella Castle. There were some amazing outfits, including a few strikingly similar to the actual Disney characters. We saw a perfect Naveen, a wonderful Cruella De Vil, and a few adorable Snow White-inspired outfits among the crowd.

While enjoying a quick lunch in Columbia Harbour House (one of my favorite quick service locations in Magic Kingdom), I met a girl who I was friends on Facebook, but hadn't met in person yet. She and her friend joined us for the rest of the day, along with one of

Meriem's hospitality coworkers from Port Orleans. Together, we vlogged in Raisa's video for Dapper Day, took pictures around the park, and met Mickey in our lovely dapper outfits.

I was having a wonderful time meeting new people, complimenting other dapper outfits, and explaining Dapper Day to curious guests in the park, but unfortunately I had to hop on the monorail and get ready for work before the big meet up on the *Liberty Belle* riverboat. From what I later saw in Raisa's video, there was quite a big turnout. There was even a baby dressed in an adorable dapper outfit, bowtie and all!

There was a final meet-up after the park closed in the Polynesian and the Grand Floridian resorts. Some of my coworkers were a little confused over all of the guests dressed in such nice clothes eating in our restaurant, but I was able to ask about their day and sometimes guess to see if they were Disneybounding as a certain character.

If you're ever in a Disney park around a specified Dapper Day, I highly recommend participating. It's a fun way to have an excuse to dress up and enjoy a day in the parks. If enough guests are in their dapper outfits, it creates a nostalgic feeling in the park, almost as if you really are back in the 1950s, expecting to see Walt walk around the corner on Main Street.

CHAPTER TWENTY-THREE

Deployed Again

After returning from Gaspy's and adjusting back to life at Capt. Cook's, I was starting to miss the people at the Grand. However, just as I was getting comfortable at Cook's again, I had a surprise on my schedule: Deployment—Art of Animation.

My stomach dropped a little when I realized where I was going. I was a little excited because Art of Animation was the newest resort in Disney World, but I had heard some not-so-appealing stories from cast members who worked at the "value" resorts. There was some good news, though. As I scrolled through my coworkers' schedules posted on the bulletin board, I noticed that at least three of my fellow interns from Cook's were going to be deployed to Art of Animation at the same time as me. Unlike my experience at the Grand Floridian, I wasn't going to be completely on my own.

Just like when I was deployed to the Grand, Liz and I took a trip before work one day to Art of Animation to fully explore the resort and my new temporary work location, the Landscapes of Flavors food court. It was rather surreal to wander around the colorful resort while remembering that just a little over a year ago I was writing about its construction on my blog. Not only was I now exploring the resort first hand, but I was going to be working there.

I went with Megan, one of my Cook's coworkers who was being deployed with me, to get our new costumes. We discovered that we had to wear a bright rainbow-patterned shirt with dark blue pants, apron, and hat. It was rather groovy, to say the least. One of my other coworkers, Carly, had already been deployed to Art of Animation when I was at the Grand Floridian. She tried her best to explain where to go to clock in and whatnot, but I learned it was much harder to locate the backstage entrance to the food court than it had been at the Grand. I spotted a lone food service worker walking toward the bus stop on his way out from his shift. I told him I was deployed and brand new to the resort, and asked whether he could show me where to clock in. He sighed, clearly exhausted from his shift, but still walked me to where I needed to be.

One aspect of Landscapes that was drastically different from Cook's and Gaspy's was its sheer size. While my two previous locations needed no more than ten cast members to fully operate, there were at least 40 cast members working at Landscapes of Flavors. Due to the massive amount of workers, this was the first restaurant to need coordinators on location, not just managers. I did cross paths and have a casual conversation with one of the managers on site during my deployment, but the majority of the time I needed to report to a coordinator in case I had any questions or concerns.

When one of the coordinators discovered I was deployed, she had the cast member I had met at the bus stop show me all the ropes, even though he was officially off the clock. I was grateful (though a little guilty) when he agreed to help me. He showed me where to clock in, where everything was stocked, where all of the cleaning supplies were located, and the various positions I would probably have during my deployment.

Since I wasn't formally trained at Landscapes, I was not allowed to work at the food stations or the cash register. In fact, as I clocked in to the computer system, I received my first assignment: trash. I'd be roaming the food court and emptying trash cans until further notice. I could already feel a yearning to return to Cook's starting to grow in my chest.

For the first three hours of my shift, I lugged a massive cart around the dining room, weaving through families and switching out trash bags to dump in a disposal backstage. Just when I thought the trash would never end, an angel from heaven arrived in the form of a cast member to send me on my break.

At the end of my too-short break, I clocked back into the computer and prayed to the Disney gods that I wouldn't be assigned trash again. My prayers were answered when I was sent to bus Route 66 (the *Cars* section of the food court) for the final three hours of my shift.

The rest of the week at Art of Animation was similar. The shifts grew a little more enjoyable each day, especially when my coworkers from Cook's worked with me at the same time. Besides taking care of the trash and bussing tables, I was also in charge of restocking the bakery and the various coolers. I always dreaded handling the coolers because they were absolutely freezing. There were extra thick black snow jackets and gloves designated for anyone who had to spend time in the coolers. Often, I had to take a break in the bakery area just so my fingers wouldn't freeze off.

Halfway through my deployment to Art, I realized I hadn't called or talked to my parents much that week. As soon as I started explaining my deployment experience to my mom and dad on the phone, I felt this overwhelming sensation of wanting to be back home. At this point, it had been over two months since I had seen my family and best friends, which was the longest time I had ever spent away from them. My family was planning on visiting the following month, but in that moment I wanted nothing more than to be back in California. I wasn't enjoying my job at Art, I was exhausted, I missed my best friend, my parents, my brother...everything.

My parents reminded me that this deployment was only temporary, and that I'll be back to enjoying my job at the Polynesian very soon. We started creating a plan for their trip in April, as well as discussed my intention to transfer schools the following semester. I felt much more at ease by the end of the conversation and realized that taking things day by day will help lessen my homesickness. With a mix of this, my family visiting, and taking a moment to ride Soarin' one day (a ride about California), I was able to rid myself of sad feelings for the rest of my program.

My experience at Art of Animation also improved. I started making new friends with my coworkers and grew more comfortable with the food court in general. I enjoyed the bakery position, because sometimes I was allowed to decorate cupcakes and cookies before putting them on display. Every hour or so, someone would clock in and get assigned a task to have all the cast members go to the center of the room with some young guests to do the "Mater Shuffle" (our version of the hokey pokey) or yell "Shark Bait! Hoo ha ha!" just like characters from *Finding Nemo*.

The dining room had the most opportunities for guest interaction. I will always remember two guests from the UK that I met during my deployment. They were two men in their sixties, and one of them had never been to a Disney park before. It was his ultimate dream to come to Walt Disney World. They asked me about places to explore in Epcot, what was the "big ball" in the center of the park (Spaceship Earth), and about the Flower and Garden Festival.

Every day when I was in the dining room I would see these two adorable old men, and they'd always remember my name and say hello. They were excited to tell me about some of the characters they'd met that day, and one even showed me his autograph book. His biggest dream was to meet Peter Pan, who I happened to stumble across near Adventureland during Dapper Day. I told him where to meet him and when. It was always a highlight of my day seeing those two and hearing about what they'd been up to.

By the end of my deployment, I was happy to return to the Polynesian. What made everything even better was being assigned to counter on my first day back, which was my favorite role. The week was starting to grow crazier each day with Spring break season quickly approaching. I was bracing myself for the hectic crowds about to arrive for the next few weeks.

CHAPTER TWENTY-FOUR

My Mortal Enemy, The "B" Bus

One factor I wish I could have changed during my program was not having a car. This was the first time since earning my license that I wasn't able to drive whenever I wanted, wherever I wanted. After quickly learning on Carmen's birthday that the buses for the college program were unreliable, my experiences with my specific bus for work (the "B" bus) continued to grow worse.

There were numerous occasions throughout my program when my bus was simply running late, causing me to nearly sprint across the Polynesian property to clock in. Every once in a while the buses were simply too late for me to make it to my shift on time; thankfully, my managers were all understanding and never reprimanded me or gave me points for being late due to the horrible bus. In fact, near the end of my program, whenever I would call one of my managers and tell them what happened, one actually joked, "Sara, why are you breaking the bus again?"

One particular day before a standard closing shift, I waited patiently at the Chatham bus stop about thirty minutes before the bus was supposed to arrive. There was another girl from the Polynesian (from merchandise) who had arrived before me waiting for the same bus. Sometimes the buses come earlier than expected, but we soon realized that we weren't going to be so lucky.

The scheduled arrival time came and went...five minutes later... ten minutes later...my heart began to race the longer we waited. I called the bus management and they insisted that it was on its way. Ten more minutes pass and I called again, this time getting a rude woman who sternly claimed, "The B bus already came to Chatham."

I kept protesting, stating that I'd been sitting here since thirty minutes prior to the arrival time, and that another girl had been waiting even longer and not a single B bus had shown up. Either this woman was lying to me, or the bus driver lied to her and told her he made it to Chatham when in reality he skipped us to catch up with the bus route schedule.

We had no choice other than to wait for the next scheduled bus. Our fingers were crossed for this one to arrive on time, but at this rate our hopes were low. Twenty minutes later, we finally saw our long-awaited "B" bus pull into the loading area and quickly hop on.

The bus took us to our usual first stop at Vista Way, but for some reason the driver left us for a few minutes without any explanation. Sometimes the drivers switched, causing us to wait at Vista Way a little longer than usual, but this wasn't one of those stops.

A few moments pass; we start growing even more anxious. Just as we were about to ask what was happening, our driver returns and asks all of us to exit the bus. My heart dropped. What the heck was going on? I was already late to work from the previous bus not showing up; what was wrong with this one?

Just as I was about to call my manager, the bus driver told us that there was something malfunctioning in his bus. We had to wait for maintenance to come and fix the problem before we were allowed to board again. At this rate, those who were on my bus en route to the Magic Kingdom for work were able to use the "A" bus that had pulled up, but the rest of us who worked at the resorts weren't blessed with this kind of option.

My manager understood the situation, but after twenty minutes of waiting we were all growing impatient. One girl started arguing with the woman in charge of the buses, who explained that they had no spare buses for us to use to get to work. The late cast member tried to persuade the woman to let us use one of the smaller vans that they take to the less populated resorts, but the woman was too stubborn to help and slammed the window on the cast member.

I was growing furious. I was already an hour late to my shift. I wasn't worried about accumulating points for my tardiness, I was just think-ing about the lack of a second cashier that my restaurant was dealing with due to my temporary absence. I understood that unfortunate events sometimes happen, but this was growing ridiculous.

Finally, after nearly thirty minutes of waiting at Vista Way, the other "B" bus pulled up to take us to our shifts. All of us Polynesian cast members started sharing how late we were to one another, and how some of them weren't as lucky to have managers waive their points on their record card for being tardy. At this rate, I was going to arrive to my shift two hours after my scheduled start time. I couldn't believe it.

As the bus was starting to get closer to our destination, the driver didn't go to the Polynesian, but actually pulled in to the Ticket and Transportation Center. The Polynesian was the usual first stop, while the TTC was supposed to be the last before returning to the apartments. We immediately started asking what was going on, and why we weren't at the right stop. The driver started arguing that the route had changed, and that the Polynesian wasn't even an option on the route anymore.

This is where I started to completely lose my patience. There was absolutely no way the Polynesian wasn't a stop on the route anymore, for there were no other buses scheduled to arrive at the resort. Not once, not ever.

The driver showed us a bus stop update flyer, which I quickly recognized as the notice for the bus stop location changing for the Grand Floridian due to construction, not the Polynesian. I explained to the driver that I just recently worked in that location, and that the Polynesian is for sure on the route. He was adamant that we were wrong, but I had at least five other Polynesian cast members behind me to defend my argument. We were all more than an hour late to our shifts, we had dealt with missing a bus, being evacuated, and fighting with the stubborn manager, and now our driver didn't know where he was going.

Never in my life have I ever wished to have my car as much as I did in that moment.

We finally convinced our driver to "make an exception" and drop us off at the Polynesian. I was sweating by the time I clocked in and made it to Capt. Cook's, explaining to my manager and all my coworkers the transportation disaster I had just experienced.

Nothing as inconvenient as that afternoon ever occurred again during my program. I was, however, skipped or forgotten after a few shifts ending at 1:30 in the morning. Front desk cast members got off of work at the same late time, so I was able to get a free cab from their manager and sometimes a ride from one of their friends back to the apartments every once in a while. Otherwise, I would be on the phone with my friends or family (thank goodness for the three hour time difference) just waiting over an hour at two in the morning for a bus that seemed to never want to show up.

One piece of advice I always recommend to those participating in the program is to bring a car. After experiencing so many close calls, being ignored, skipped, arriving late, and hearing others getting stuck on the road, I always warn future college program participants of the risks with relying on the buses. I understand that some people are in the same situation that I was, living too far away to drive to their internship and bring their car, but if it's possible, do it. You don't want to end up in any of the massively inconvenient situations I and many other cast members had to experience.

CHAPTER TWENTY-FIVE

Decisions

About halfway through my program, I was still shocked that the DCP was my life. I would sometimes have moments alone where I would sit and just think about where I was and what I was doing. Not everyone has the opportunity to live their dream, and I was cherishing every precious second.

With this in mind, I had many important decisions to make for when my program ended. Many of my friends already knew they wanted to apply to extend their program and stay during the summer, possibly try a different role, or go seasonal and work a certain number of hours throughout the year. Part of me was tempted to extend and try for one of my preferred roles such as merchandise or attractions, but I knew it was best for me to keep my current ending date and go back home for the summer.

I was in the middle of transferring colleges after finishing my education at community college. I needed to choose which school I wanted to transfer to after the summer. Did I want to go somewhere closer to home? How about moving to southern California? Or did I want to stay in Florida?

After a few months of living here, I realized that even though I loved my life at Walt Disney World, Florida was just too far away from home. This left me with two options: go to a college 15 minutes away from home, or take a chance and move to a school in southern California.

When I pictured myself living back home after this amazing adventure, I couldn't imagine myself happy. Even though I'd love to be right near my family and childhood friends, I've always known that I needed to branch out of my small town to pursue my goals. One tempting factor about southern California was Disneyland. If I attended the university I was accepted into down south, I could potentially become a Disney cast member once again. The school

I was leaning toward was also well known for my major; it had an amazing business program. With all of this in mind and discussing all the various options with my family, we came to the clear conclusion that I needed to attend school in southern California.

After excitedly accepting my offer to California State University, Fullerton, I received an email about applications opening for potential future DCP campus representatives. I had heard about campus reps before and knew that I wanted to be one of them. Disney campus reps were DCP alumni who were representing the college program at their university. Essentially, the campus rep is the in-person source of information for prospective students who want to apply for the Disney College Program. I promoted the program on my blog on a daily basis, so why not become an official representative for Disney at my new school?

Both Sara and I filled out the first step of the application to become reps at our new schools, fingers crossed that the results would be promising. In the meantime, there was no point in worrying about what might happen. We still had the rest of our program to enjoy together, and plenty of items on our bucket list to complete before we traveled back home.

CHAPTER TWENTY-SIX

Exploring My Future

Interns participating in the Disney College Program have the option to attend various classes throughout their program. Subjects range from personal branding, engineering, security, entertainment, business, and more. Students aren't required to take classes, but some colleges offer credit for taking one or two of them. Since I was in between schools, I knew I wasn't going to receive any credit for taking classes during my program. However, I couldn't pass up the opportunity to take Exploring Marketing, a class that explored every aspect of Disney's marketing department, since marketing is my major. Some classes require textbooks and homework assignments, but my class was part of an "exploration series", which meant no homework.

Bethany registered for the same class, which started about a month or so into our program. Throughout the three-month class, cast members from different marketing departments came in to explain their roles and the responsibilities of their departments. After the introductory session, we learned about Disney's national and global marketing campaigns, branding, marketing for special events, Disney vacation club sales, Disney cruise line marketing, as well as consumer relationship marketing.

Each week brought interesting discussions, important information, group activities, and networking opportunities. In addition, we often reviewed past marketing campaigns such as commercials, pamphlets, emails, and themed promotions.

A couple of my favorite lessons were about branding and special events. For one class, our guest speaker explored the power behind Disney's brand, and how they use this brand to their advantage when promoting certain aspects of their theme parks, resorts, and attractions. My favorite in-class activity came during the lesson about special events. Each group needed to brainstorm and create a special event for one of the Disney parks and how we were going to market it. My group had the idea to dedicate a week where Future World in Epcot transformed into a world dedicated to candy, similar to the Sugar Rush game from *Wreck-It Ralph*. For a limited time, we would convert Test Track to an actual Sugar Rush-themed attraction, as well as create and include a parade, since Epcot was the only park without one at the time. Our teacher and guest speaker loved our idea.

Hearing about current cast members who worked in Disney's business and marketing department after participating in the Disney College Program was inspiring. The DCP held special events and meet and greets specifically for current college program participants to ask questions and network with select DCP alumni cast members who now work full-time for the company. These were called CPASS events. I attended the one scheduled with Disney's social media and marketing department. I learned how some DCP alumni returned to the company and moved forward with their careers as cast members and heard their advice for my possible future marketing career path. Whether you're hoping to be involved with Disney's business department, entertainment, training and development, or anything else, you should make sure to attend some of these events. You never know who you might meet and what you might learn that could make a difference in where your career takes you.

I learned an incredible amount through my class and events like CPASS. In fact, the Exploring Marketing class was one reason why I chose to participate in the Disney World program, since they don't offer it in California. The class enlightened me to the many opportunities within the company, which came in quite handy later.

CHAPTER TWENTY-SEVEN

Water Park Adventures

The weather started to warm up around halfway through my program, which motivated me to finally visit Disney's two water parks: Blizzard Beach and Typhoon Lagoon. First on my list was traveling to Blizzard with Sara and Liz.

Our afternoon was filled with numerous water slides, floating along the lazy river, and climbing many, many stairs. This was my first time to the water park, but I recognized the ever-daunting Summit Plummit (one of the largest and steepest water slides I've ever seen) as well as the children's adventure area, where kids could climb across floating icebergs and swing down on a zip line into a pool. I remembered the children's area from an old Disney Parks sing-a-long video I would watch when I was very little. I was always so jealous of the kids in the movie; they always looked like they were having so much fun.

The lazy river was my favorite area of the park. The three of us found an inner tube and relaxed in the water under the sunshine for almost an hour, slowly drifting around the park. Occasionally, we would say hi to some of the lifeguards, or squeal and attempt to dodge some of the various spurts of chilly water from the ski-lodge themed decorations. Sara and I danced with the idea of conquering Summit Plummit, but then decided that braving the drop was for another day.

We were all starving by the time we left the park, so we took a detour to Steak 'n' Shake. I had a simple hamburger, fries, and a mint chocolate chip milkshake. It definitely hit the spot after a full day in the sun.

A couple days later, after I had my Exploring Marketing class in the early morning, I journeyed to Typhoon Lagoon with my friend Jake. Jake worked in custodial in Hollywood Studios, and we met on Facebook before our programs began. Since he lived just a few buildings down from my classroom, I simply walked to his place before heading over to the water park.

As soon as we walked through the entrance to Typhoon, I could tell that I was going to fall in love with this park. Many of my friends would tell me that they preferred Blizzard Beach and found Typhoon rather boring in comparison, but I have to disagree. Blizzard may have more water slides, but one look at Typhoon's massive wave pool and you'll know why I prefer it.

I also preferred the decorations and theme. While Blizzard's theme and story is about a water park that was created in a random freak winter storm, Typhoon was more tropical, including thick shrubbery and trees. I felt more immersed into the storm-ravaged theme and world of Typhoon Lagoon. Plus, it also helps that I simply love tropical landscapes and settings in general.

Jake and I first experienced the wave pool, which was crazy fun. I've never really considered myself a wave pool kind of person, but this one changed my mind. We tested a few of the larger waves, which occasionally swept me off my feet and pulled me underwater when I wasn't bracing myself. The waves here can grow so large that guests can take surfing lessons inside the wave pool. These lessons were on my bucket list when I started my program, but I realized that I couldn't afford it.

We quickly deciphered that the biggest waves occurred after what sounded like an emergency alarm. With this in mind, we swam out to the deepest part of the pool, treading water and waiting patiently to hear the loud horns go off. Just when my legs were starting to grow a little fatigued, the alarm filled the area, making all the guests shriek with glee. Jake and I turned to face the beach, bracing for the six-foot waves. Pretty soon, we heard a giant *thump* from behind the wall, and we're immediately lifted and soaring through the water straight toward the shore. Whenever I visited the ocean, I was too afraid to ride the dangerous waves. At Typhoon, I learned that it's actually a lot of fun. We allowed the waves to push us all the way to shore, dodging guests here and there as we went. After catching our breath for a few minutes, we swam back out to the deep end to repeat our daring dance with the waves until we were too exhausted to continue.

Next we ventured our way to one of the water slides, Crushin' Gusher. The slides are themed off of an abandoned fruit-processing plant, which was operating before the massive typhoon hit the park. Banana Blaster, Coconut Crusher, and Pineapple Plunger are the three slides we tackled, twisting, turning, and dropping along the way. My personal favorite was Banana Blaster, which is ironic because I absolutely despise bananas.

Up next was the shark reef. I was nervous because I'm a little scared of fish, but I knew there was nothing I needed to be worried about. Jake and I grabbed a goggles and snorkels and patiently waited with a group at the water's edge for further instructions.

"Once I tell you, you are all going to slowly move forward and swim directly ahead, not stopping or diving at any time," the lifeguard lectured. He mentioned a few more pointers and answered a couple questions before giving us the green light. "Okay everyone good luck finding Dory!"

I was giggling to myself as I eased into the chilly salt water. I placed the snorkel in my mouth and slowly dipped my head under the surface, introducing myself to the colorful aquatic world beneath my toes. Cute little clownfish, looming sharks, and other sea creatures danced below as I gently swam above the reef. I felt comfortable with the distance between the fish and me, but as we grew closer to the other side of the pool, two angular silver fish with large square heads started to creep toward me, swimming a little too close for comfort. Jake said the same fish swam strangely near him as well, which means they were definitely accustomed to humans poking around their turf.

We made it to the end of the pool to return our snorkel gear. We were now famished, so we found a couple of chairs on the beach near the wave pool and took turns getting food to save our spots. While I was waiting in line to order my lunch, I noticed from her nametag that the cast member helping take orders was from a city I recognized in northern California. I started to chat with her and told her that I was also from the area. When I told her my city, her eyes lit up. "That's where I went to college!"

My mouth dropped. "No way! Are you doing the college program here?"

"Yes, I am! Are you?"

"Yes!"

Not only did we come from the same part of the state, but it turns out she was also staying in Patterson Court. She drove with a few friends from the same area in California all the way to Florida, which to me sounded absolutely insane. On the bright side, she didn't have to deal with the buses. We talked until my food was ready, wished each other the best of luck for the rest of our program, and hoped we'd run into each other again soon. Sadly, that was the last time I saw her, but it was definitely wonderful to meet by chance another fellow northern Californian.

Jake and I spent the rest of the afternoon tanning in the beach area, singing along to the *Fantasmic!* soundtrack on his phone, and swimming in the wave pool one last time. The water parks were a refreshing new way to spend days off during my program, especially since I had never been to either of them before. I highly recommend that college program interns take advantage of the free admission into the water parks while it lasts, because once peak season hits in the summertime, you'll have to buy discounted tickets instead of going in for free.

When the park closed, Jake drove me to Art of Animation so I could check my family into their hotel room. They were at that very moment flying into Orlando to spend time with me for a few days for the first time since my program. We were staying in a *Lion King* suite, which I was excited about since *The Lion King* is my all-time favorite Disney movie.

The day they were arriving at the hotel was coincidentally my younger brother's birthday, so before they arrived I spent time decorating the room with balloons, streamers, and "Happy Birthday!" banners as a surprise. Just as I was tying the last balloon, I heard a knock on the door.

My family was finally here!

CHAPTER TWENTY-EIGHT

Family Vacation

As I opened the door, my mom pushed through my dad and brother and demanded to receive the first hug. I hugged the rest of my family and then led my brother into the hotel room, showing him my surprise. My mom and dad's birthdays had occurred during the months after I had moved, so I also had some late birthday present surprises wrapped in cute little bags on the bed. The day before they arrived I went to Downtown Disney and found the perfect shirts for each of them: a basketball-themed Mickey Mouse shirt for my dad, a pink Minnie Mouse shirt for my mom, and a dark blue Walt Disney World Resort shirt for my brother.

After more hugs and some catching up, we were all simply exhausted from their long hours of traveling and my full day in the sun at the water park. Our plan was to wake up early and head straight to Hollywood Studios, since it had many of our favorite rides. One great thing I love about my family is that they'll all go on any ride I recommend or want to try in a theme park. The only attraction my mom doesn't particularly care for is Tower of Terror. She'll ride it every once in a while, but one time during a vacation is enough for her.

The next morning the scuffling of feet and running shower water reminded me to wake up and start getting ready to go. However, when I turned over on my side to get up, my muscles ached. At first, I thought I might have just been sore from all the swimming and treading water from the day before, but my prediction changed as soon as I tried to take a drink. My throat felt scratchy and hot against the cool water.

I was sick.

I had yet to get sick in Florida, and yet the one time my immune system decided to fail on me was when my family flew across the country to visit. I wasn't going to let my annoying illness ruin the short amount of time I had with them, so we packed our things and headed out to the buses, onward to Hollywood Studios.

We made a beeline to Toy Story Midway Mania, where by some miracle it was only a 25-minute wait. (It's usually at least an hour or more.) My dad had never experienced this attraction before, so I was curious about how he was going to like it. He and I can be rather competitive with each other, so this was perfect for the two of us to experience together.

It was fun watching my brother out of the corner of my eye shoot like a madman at the screen while I fired away trying to score my own points. I kept my undefeated record, and my father scored the most pathetic amount of points I've ever seen. I was surprised; usually my dad is better at these kinds of games. Turns out, he thought we had a limited amount of ammo during the game, even though at the beginning one of the characters says, "You have an unlimited amount of ammo, so shoot as much as you want!" To this day, the three of us have never stopped teasing him about his little misunderstanding.

My dad insisted on a rematch in the future now that he knows there's no shot limit, which meant snatching a few FastPasses before heading over to Rock 'n' Roller Coaster and Tower of Terror. Once we finished Coaster, the weather was growing warmer and my sickness was starting to catch up to me. We decided to head back to the hotel for a little bit so I could escape the heat and rest. My family was still a little worn out from traveling the day before, and they were just fine with the idea of relaxing before returning to the park.

Back at our hotel room, I was able to nap for about an hour and wake up refreshed just as the weather was beginning to cool down. My parents went to the food court to pick up some lunch before we returned to the Studios for the rest of the night. We used our FastPasses for Toy Story, and this time my dad was much closer to the rest of our scores (even though I still held my title as undefeated champion).

Disney certainly knows how to bring out the inner child of my dad. Not only did he completely fall in love with Toy Story Midway Mania, but also the entire time we were in Studios he would not stop asking whether we could ride Tower of Terror again.

"You know what's a good idea? Tower of Terror."

"Do you think we can fit in another Tower ride?"

"I think the best ride here is definitely Tower. Coaster is good, but there's just something about Tower that makes it great."

There's no doubt that I'm his daughter.

At the end of the night, I received a text from Mitch telling me he was working at Coaster. While my parents saved us a spot at Fantasmic!, my brother and I squeezed in one last Aerosmith run and saw Mitch in his element. When we returned to my parents, we were informed that Fantasmic! was going to be cancelled due to inclement weather. We were slightly bummed, but we were ready to head back to the hotel and call it a night.

I loved spending time with my family for the next two days. I almost fully recovered from my small bout of sickness after a second, more relaxing day in Epcot. It was fun being their tour guide and telling them fun stories and about memories I had made in certain areas of the parks with my new friends. I'm happy we had time to show them my beautiful Polynesian Resort and Capt. Cook's. My family met a handful of my coworkers and I even witnessed their first Dole Whip experience (which they loved).

Our last day consisted entirely of the Magic Kingdom, going on some of our favorite rides, introducing them to New Fantasyland, and finishing our little family vacation watching Celebrate the Magic, the Main Street Electric Parade, and of course, Wishes. Just as I was explaining to my family my love for the donkey boys during the Electric Parade, one of the donkeys popped out of nowhere to interact with my brother, who had been looking off into the distance while leaning on a trashcan. While I had spent three months trying to get their attention, literally all my brother needed to do was space out and look away. Typical.

I woke up on my last day with my family with a heavy heart. This was the only time they were visiting me during my program, so we weren't reuniting until I moved back home.

We ate one last breakfast in Landscapes of Flavors, packed everything up, and walked to the airport buses in front of the hotel. My family's shuttle arrived as Jake was pulling up to take me back to my apartment. It was hard to say goodbye, but I was incredibly thankful that they were able to visit at least once during my program. We had an amazing little family vacation that week, and I was excited to see them again back home in May.

But first, I still had just less than two months in Florida. Right now I needed to focus on my program and make the most of the time I had left with the amazing people I had met so far in this amazing place.

CHAPTER TWENTY-NINE

Miracle Day and Endless Pie

I had an extra day off after my family flew back home before I returned to work. I wasn't quite sure what to do, since many of my friends were working or already had plans. I figured it had been too long since I had spent time with Christine, so I shot her a text and the next thing we knew we were in Hollywood Studios for my third visit that week.

Since it was a Monday, the park was wonderfully empty. The miracles began when we walked by Toy Story and saw a 40-minute wait in the middle of the day. In fact, all of the lines were hardly any wait! We ended up riding Tower of Terror probably around four or five times in a row.

We sat next to interesting and hilariously entertaining people each time, especially these two female guests who had never been on Tower of Terror before. They were freaking out all the way from the beginning in the library to when they were actually in the elevators experiencing the attraction. The entire time they were on the ride they were hugging each other in complete and utter terror, screaming, "OH LORD WHY?! NO! NO, NO, NO! THIS IS HORRIBLE! NEVER AGAIN!!" Christine and I couldn't even attempt to pose for a photo during our ride with these two, because we couldn't compose ourselves from laughing so hard.

Throughout the day, we started to notice a strange theme each time we were grouped onto an attraction. For some reason, every single time we rode a ride we were placed in the same row. Star Tours? Row four. Tower of Terror? Row four. Toy Story? Row four. Great Movie Ride? Row four. It got to the point that whenever the cast member asked us, "How many in your party?" we predicted we'd be placed in row four. From this day forward, every time one of us is placed in the fourth row on an attraction, we take a picture of the number and send it to the other person. I'm now always excited when I'm placed in row four; it's become our little inside joke.

Later in the afternoon we were beginning to grow hungry. We brainstormed some ideas for lunch, but agreed that we weren't really in the mood for any of the quick service restaurants. Even though we didn't have reservations, Christine and I decided on 50's Prime Time Café. It was worth a shot to see if they had any tables open, especially since the park was dead.

Sure enough, when we asked the host if they had any available tables for two, we were seated immediately. I hadn't eaten at 50's Prime Time since my birthday, so I was excited to try the food one more time. I was also curious about whether our waitress was going to play her role a little better than the slightly disappointing waitress we had back in February.

Our waitress approached our table and introduced herself as Cousin May. After asking us about our day and if we wanted anything to drink, she questioned, "Now, you haven't been hanging out with the Joneses next door, have you? I've heard that Indiana character gets into quite a bit of trouble."

She was referring to the Indiana Jones Epic Stunt Show Spectacular right next to the restaurant, which made us laugh. Christine and I guaranteed that we weren't associating with the Joneses, especially Indiana. We wouldn't want to find ourselves in any kind of predicament.

Just like before, our food didn't disappoint. I had the fried chicken again, and Christine had the pot pie. Our waitress made a few more jokes and puns here and there throughout our meal, which kept us entertained. She was definitely more into character than the last waitress we had.

We said goodbye to Cousin May as we paid for our food, and ended the night riding Tower of Terror (in row four) over and over again. We tried for a new personal record for consecutive rides, which I think amounted to around five or six times in a row. If I hadn't memorized the video in the library scene by that point, I learned it word for word by the end of the night.

After this amazing Miracle Day, Christine and I agreed that we needed to hang out again very soon. A couple weeks later, I was talking to one of my coworkers at the bus stop and she mentioned something about the Great American Pie Festival in a town near Orlando. Apparently, at this festival you can eat endless amounts of pie for only 10 dollars.

Bottomless pie? Count me in! I asked Christine whethe she was free before one of my shifts during one of the days of the festival, and she agreed to join in on the pie without a moment of hesitation.

Christine and I left bright and early for the short drive to Celebration. It was strange venturing outside Disney for a reason other than grocery shopping or Universal Studios. While we followed the GPS on my phone, it almost seemed like we were driving into the middle of nowhere. The only scenery on the freeway during our journey was dark green, flat landscape, and marshlands. Not a single building appeared. After around 30 minutes of driving, we made a couple of turns down some streets and heard my phone say, "You have arrived at your destination."

We were in the middle of nowhere.

It looked like my phone had taken us to a model home community, not the bustling American Pie Festival. There were maybe one or two cars within this empty, simple neighborhood with the identical landscaping in each front yard. Without a doubt, we were completely lost. Christine immediately pulled out her own GPS, entered in the address to the festival, and turned back onto the freeway. I was worried that after spending so much time driving to this random empty community that we wouldn't have enough time to enjoy the festival before I had to leave for work. I did my best to push the thought out of my head as we made our way to the real location of the festival. After all, endless pie was waiting for us.

Thirty more minutes of driving later, we found ourselves in an absolutely adorable town. Downtown Celebration was filled with cute, old-fashioned, pastel-colored buildings surrounding a beautiful lake with a surface so smooth it resembled glass. We parked and walked around the lake toward the festival, which was filled with numerous fellow pie lovers. We bought our wristbands and immediately started to make a dent at the free stands.

Each booth contained various flavors of pie sponsored directly from certain grocery stores or markets from around the area. We grabbed as many kinds as we could, even flavors we had never heard of before. Apple, pumpkin, blackberry, chocolate, coconut cream...the list was endless. Christine and I also managed to snag a few packets of frosting mix found scattered in buckets around the festival. We were sweating from the heat as we grabbed the last bit of our loot and found a place in the shade to enjoy our delicious dessert. Every single piece was delightful, although we were filled to the brim by our last bite. We wanted to go back for seconds, but our stomachs were protesting. Instead, we relaxed and talked until it was time to go back to Disney for my shift.

It was nice exploring outside of Disney property, and I wish I had taken the opportunity to explore even more during my program. It's so easy to grow comfortable in the Disney bubble and forget that there's more to experience in Florida besides theme parks and Universal Studios. One place I regret not visiting was the beach. Granted, I've been to beaches before in my life, but I wish I had spent time at a beach in Florida with the fantastic friends I had made during my program. Every time we tried to make plans to go, the weather wouldn't cooperate or they simply would fall through.

Take advantage of the opportunities you have during your program. It's not every day that you get to live in Florida with incredible people and make magic daily. During the last two months of my program, Sara and I made sure we conquered as much on our bucket list as possible. If you make a bucket list, use it. Don't regret not doing something when you have the chance. I'm thankful that Christine was willing to spontaneously drive to a new town for a pie festival we had only just heard about. We often reminisce about the day we were always thrown into row four, or that one time we found ourselves in a random model home community. They were two of my all-time favorite days during my program, and I'm so thankful that Tumblr and the DCP brought friends like Christine and others into my life.

CHAPTER THIRTY

Life at Capt. Cook's

Even though a day off in the parks was always fun, most of the time you would find me working at Cook's. I started to grow closer to my coworkers a little later on during my program. I couldn't have imagined working with better people, which is a blessing since we were with each other for eight hours a day, five days a week.

The three girls I was the closest to were Carly, Megan, and Nideria. Some of our managers would occasionally joke about how it was dangerous to have the four of us working together during the same shift. Every time we saw that we all had the same schedule, we'd praise to the heavens because we knew it was going to be a fun shift. I'll always remember constantly quoting *Pitch Perfect* with the girls while we were working together at the counter, the cash register, or in the dining room.

Another amazing friend I made at work was an International College Program student from Brazil named Rodolpho. He came to Capt. Cook's a little later into my program, but quickly became part of our little ohana. One afternoon while we were working, Rodolpho turned to me and said, "You know who you look like?"

I shook my head, puzzled.

"You remind me of Anne Hathaway."

From that moment on, he'd refer to me as Anne.

My non-college program coworkers were great to work with, too. One part-time cast member, Nick, became a good friend during and after the program. We both would geek out at work over everything Harry Potter and Marvel, specifically how excited we were for *Iron Man 3* to premiere in the last month of my program. The culinary team was one of the main reasons why I loved counter. Some of them teased me whenever I had an airhead moment or if I was a little clumsy (I'm definitely a klutz every once in a while). They asked about California, what it was like, and the differences between

Disneyland and Walt Disney World. This was actually a common question I received from guests.

One rather slow night, I was on dining room wiping down tables and organizing chairs before the end of my shift. I walked by two guests at one table; both huddled over to watch a video on a phone. I peeked over one of their shoulders to glance at what video they were watching and nearly gasped with excitement.

"Are you watching World of Color?" I couldn't contain myself. Hardly anyone in Florida had seen World of Color before, or had even been to Disneyland in general.

The one holding the phone turned to me and smiled, "Yes! It's such an amazing show! Have you seen it?"

I laughed, "Have I *seen* it? It's only everything that's good in this world and more!"

"That's what I'm trying to tell my friend!" He jokingly nudged the other man at the table, who shyly chuckled to him. "There's nothing here that's as good as World of Color."

"I couldn't agree more." At this rate, I knew I was going to love this guest. "I'm actually from California. I love Disneyland and that show so much."

He turned to me and said: "I was just explaining how Disney World is so different in comparison to Disneyland..."

"...But you can only compare it to Magic Kingdom, which isn't as good as Disneyland," I exclaimed.

"I totally agree!!"

We continued to excitedly discuss more of the details between the two parks: how Space Mountain was better in Disneyland, that Haunted Mansion was better here in Florida, and that Florida has a leg up with Celebrate the Magic and the Electric Parade. The two of us agreed on absolutely everything when it came to comparing the two parks. We basically became best friends.

Sadly, I had to get back to work and the two guests were heading back to their rooms, so I wished them a good rest of their vacation and he told me he hopes I can see World of Color again some time soon. Experiences similar to this one always brightened my day. I loved meeting people from around the world, who all came together for the purpose of enjoying the parks and spending time with their friends or family. You'd be surprised by how much you can improve a cast member's shift with a simple conversation. I loved hearing about guests' vacations, what rides they rode, the food they ate, what they liked and didn't like. It was especially a treat to hear children grow excited when I asked them about their favorite rides or the characters they had met. Their eyes light up and they never want to stop telling me their stories, even if their parents are slowly nudging and hinting that they needed to leave.

Along with hearing about guests' vacations, I also loved giving them tips and advice about what they should do and look for at each park. Since I went to the parks so often on my days off, I slowly began to learn the best times and places to watch the shows and parades, which FastPasses to get first, and which attractions certain types of people might enjoy. Guests were usually grateful for the advice, and knowing that I was able to help them with their vacations was a great feeling.

Our Capt. Cook's ohana ventured together outside of work every once in a while. Since Nick also worked at Universal Studios, he was able to bring the three girls and Rodolpho into the parks on the same day I was already going with Liz and her best friend from home. We all ended up meeting with each other in Islands of Adventure, exploring Wizarding World, and goofing around in the Universal Studios side of the resort. It was nice spending time together outside of those hideous costumes and away from the fried food every so often. Nick even tried to convince me to buy a wand for myself, which I refused due to the fact that I knew it'd be hard to fit into a suitcase on the plane back home.

We spontaneously decided to attempt to conquer a Kitchen Sink at Beaches 'n' Cream after we left Universal Studios. The Kitchen Sink is an enormous ice cream sundae that includes ten scoops of ice cream, every topping you can imagine, and a whole can of whipped cream.

A WHOLE CAN??

That's right. A whole can.

It was almost tradition to attempt to eat an entire Kitchen Sink with friends during your college program. I had conquered it once before with a different group of friends, but this time the Cook's crew needed to give it a shot.

We had a strong start, but slowly started to fade about halfway through. The six of us (Nick and Rodolpho didn't participate) had already eaten dinner that night, so our stomachs weren't completely empty or prepared for ten scoops of ice cream. We finished about two-thirds of the sundae, completely unable to continue any longer.

Unfortunately, the Kitchen Sink conquered us.

CHAPTER THIRTY-ONE

Happy Birthday, Animal Kingdom!

On a cloudy Earth Day in April, Sara and I attended Animal Kingdom's 15th anniversary. Some guests were lined up at the park entrance hours before the park was even open, all to have a chance to buy some of the special edition anniversary merchandise. Sara and I were only interested in the limited 15th anniversary button, which a cast member simply handed to us as soon as we walked through the turnstiles.

We pinned the giant yellow and brown 15 on our shirts and grabbed a couple of special edition Animal Kingdom park maps on our way to meet with one of Sara's work friends. We saw that the line for special anniversary merchandise was at least two hours long! Instead of spending our morning waiting in line for a shirt, we began our day with a trip down the Pangani Forest Trail, where Sara knew someone who was doing a professional internship. While on the trail, we were surrounded by colorful birds, observed giant hippos, laughed with playful monkeys, and even saw a mother gorilla watching over her sleeping baby less than two feet away from us.

When we exited the trail, we noticed that our roommate Sarah was working at the entrance for the Kilimanjaro Safaris. We said hi and decided to ride, since there really wasn't a long line. One reason why I love this attraction is because no safari is ever the same.

We journeyed out of Africa to visit Asia and ride Expedition Everest once before going to see Finding Nemo: The Musical for the first time. It was a different experience seeing *Finding Nemo* as a musical, and I had to adjust to all of the puppeteers. Even though I find the show cute and the songs catchy, it's not one I'll go out of my way to see multiple times. However, the puppets were beautiful and the woman who portrayed Dory was absolutely perfect.

Sara was getting hungry, so we decided that it was time for lunch at Pizzafari. To our delight, the restaurant was having a cookie decorating area in honor of the park's anniversary! The four of us each decorated one butterfly shaped sugar cookie with blue, pink, and yellow frosting colors and crazy sprinkles. By the time we finished decorating, we had frosting all over our fingers and sprinkles scattered on our table and laps. It was quite a colorful and delicious mess!

After devouring our beautiful butterfly cookies, it was time to return to Everest. To our surprise, the line was ridiculously short even though it was the park's anniversary. We took advantage of it and rode ten times in a row. Each round on the attraction consisted of the best and craziest ride photos, concluding with each of us holding up ten fingers to showcase our new personal record for consecutive rides on any attraction.

When we finished our tenth and final round on Everest, we discovered that Animal Kingdom was scheduled to close in a few minutes. We raced to the other side of the park and quickly rode DINOSAUR. As we walked through the queue filled with artifacts of dinosaur bones and ancient species, we noticed that the line was virtually non-existent, just like all the lines had been that afternoon. By the time we made it to the room with the video about the safety instructions, we were hit with a wave of fatigue. We plopped onto the carpet and nearly fell asleep during the safety video, which we had probably seen at least 50 times by that point during our program. The cast members working the attraction started giggling when other guests started to follow our lead by camping out on the ground during the film. Many of the guests also loved the photo we took during the ride, which we made sure was grotesquely unflattering. One man who went on the ride alone in our car actually bought himself a copy of the picture!

Animal Kingdom was sadly closed by the time we exited DINOSAUR, but to this day I believe that celebrating its 15th anniversary was one of the best and most memorable experiences I had in the parks during my program. It had been a little while since Sara and I spent quality time together due to our crazy work schedules, and it was wonderful meeting and getting to know two of her friends.

Sara and I ended the night watching our favorite chick flick, *Something Borrowed*, back in our apartment before it was time for me to get some sleep ahead of an early morning shift back at Cook's the next day. While we were watching the film we realized just how little time we had left in Florida before we'd have to return to reality. In one short month, we would resume our old lives in California, and we weren't ready. We didn't want this life to end.

CHAPTER THIRTY-TWO

Starlight Splash

Near the end of each college program semester, Disney throws either a formal or a giant pool party for its interns, depending on the time of the year. During my spring program, Disney threw a massive swim party in Typhoon Lagoon, solely for DCP cast members, called Starlight Splash. I was thrilled that a coworker was willing to take my shift that night so I could attend. I met up with Meriem and her room-mates to drive over to Typhoon after the park was closed for guests.

When we arrived, we could hear music pumping from the beach as cast members in charge of the party gave us free glow-in-the-dark Starlight Splash t-shirts. They had a DJ on the beach right next to the wave pool with activities and competitions for free DCP merchandise. I snagged a Disney Interns wristband that was thrown into the crowd while I was waiting for my friends to put their belongings away in the lockers. We all adventured into the wave pool, which was a different experience with popular music thumping through the park. At one point, they even started to play Spice Girls and the theme song from "Fresh Prince of Bel-Air", which made me ridiculously excited.

I ran into Christine a couple hours into the party, and she joined the rest of us as we walked to the available water slides. We were all still enjoying the night even though clouds were rolling it and it began sprinkling. It was fun experiencing water slides at night in the rain. While we were enjoying the slides, fireworks started exploding and crackling near the beach. The theme song from *Pirates of the Caribbean* began playing as the flares danced and glittered in the cloudy sky.

It was around time for dinner when the fireworks ended, so we made our way to the area where they were serving endless free food (even the ice cream that guests buy in the parks). As we made our way to the tables, we noticed pirates walking around on the beach. I'm still kicking myself because Captain Jack Sparrow made a rare appearance for pictures and I didn't even know.

I found Carly, Nideria, and Megan out on the dance floor on the beach. Christine and I joined them to dance the rest of the night away on the sand. Every once in a while they'd continue to toss random free Disney Internship merchandise into the crowd. It was wonderful to simply let loose and have fun with some of my friends. Not many people can say they experienced Typhoon Lagoon at night, much less a pirate-themed beach party complete with fireworks and free Mickey Premium Bars. It was a night I will never forget, all thanks to the Disney College Program.

CHAPTER THIRTY-THREE

Goofy's Mystery Tour and Disneybound Day

Each year, Walt Disney World hosts a special cast member-only event in Hollywood Studios called Goofy's Mystery Tour. The event is one giant scavenger hunt around the Streets of America for cast members and their friends and family. Registration is extremely competitive, but Meriem was able to snag a spot for our team of four, which included Liz, Sara, and the two of us.

Since the Mystery Tour didn't start until 10 pm, we decided it was time for us to get a group together to "Disneybound" and go character hunting around the parks. We all had the perfect outfits: I was Snow White, Sara was Marie from *The Aristocats*, Meriem was Princess Jasmine, Sydney was Rapunzel, and Liz was Pocahontas. Quite a few guests and cast members recognized that we were dressed as Disney characters. It was fun to see if they could guess each of our characters.

We started our day in Epcot, immediately heading to the German pavilion to wait in line for Snow White. Our goal was to meet as many of our characters as possible; depending on how much time we had during the day before we needed to leave for Goofy's Mystery Tour. Sara, Liz, and I were first in line for Snow, while the other girls in our group went to Morocco to wait in line for Aladdin and Jasmine. While we were waiting, it started to sprinkle. I was growing a little worried that Snow wasn't going to come out and visit guests because of the rain, but fortunately she found a little section under the roof where we could take pictures together without getting wet.

My interaction with Snow was rather lackluster. She simply asked how my day was going and didn't acknowledge my outfit (which was identical to hers) until right before we took a photo. She only mentioned, "Oh, I love your outfit!" and posed with me for the picture. Our meet and greet with Jasmine and Aladdin was much more interesting.

Immediately, Aladdin and Jasmine noticed a pattern with our outfits. Jasmine tried to name everyone's character, but had trouble with Sara's.

"Hmm...who do you think she is, Aladdin?"

He scratched his head. "Aurora?"

We shook our heads and gave them a hint: "She's an animal!"

They were still stumped.

"She's Marie, from *The Aristocats*!" Meriem piped in.

"Oh!! I see it!" Aladdin exclaimed. (This was how many of our character visits and interactions with cast members went whenever they'd try and guess who we were.)

After Meriem posed with Aladdin and Jasmine alone, Jasmine arranged a group photo and had all of us pose just like each of our characters. It turned into one of my favorite pictures for the day. We continued through Epcot and made our way to Magic Kingdom to meet and take photos with Rapunzel, Marie, and a few other princesses. The rain began to fade, which allowed us to have our own mini photo shoots in the Morocco Pavilion in Epcot and in front of Cinderella Castle in Magic Kingdom.

With our picture session finished, we ventured to Hollywood Studios to check in to Goofy's Mystery Tour. We were one of the last teams to arrive, but made it just in time before the festivities began. Many other teams were also dressed in correlating or matching outfits, including characters from *Monsters Inc., The Wizard of Oz*, and other famous movies.

We were directed to the Lights, Motors, Action! set where a DJ was blasting music for a sea of dancing cast members in the stands. Liz, Sara, Meriem, and I managed to sit right next to a team of extremely enthusiastic middle-aged women who were a little *too* into dancing along to the DJ's tunes. They were really getting into the YMCA and screaming at any opportunity. Their cheering even continued during the first part of the competition, which grew a bit irritating, but we tried to make the best of the situation.

The first part of Goofy's Mystery Tour was a massive set of trivia questions. I was excited about this portion because I absolutely love Disney trivia. Some of the questions were rather easy, such as, "What date did Magic Kingdom open?" (October 1, 1971) while other questions were a little trickier, like "Who has the fastest horse, the prettiest sister, the surest rifle, and the ugliest dog in Texas?" (Davy

Crockett) We actually answered more than 70% correctly. We were rather impressed!

Round two was completely different. Team members were tied together by bungees on belt loops and given a puzzle with some clues along with instructions on who to find once each team solved their first puzzle. The ultimate goal was to solve a total of 15 puzzles by the end of the night. Each correctly solved puzzle would reveal a letter to help solve the main question for the scavenger hunt. The team with the most correctly finished puzzles and a correct final answer for the big question would win the tour.

Our first puzzle was about a table setup for a science fair. Each science fair participant had specific rules about who they sat next to, which direction they were facing in comparison to others, etc. It took us longer than we expected to figure everything out, but after we arranged each booth in our assumed correct order, we had to find a group of convention geeks who were mingling somewhere in Hollywood Studios. We walked all around the Streets of America trying to find these nerds, and on the way we spotted *Twilight* super fans, characters from *Wreck-It Ralph*'s "Sugar Rush", some mad scientists, and many more odd and wacky individuals. We finally found our convention crew, who approved our set-up solution and gave us our next puzzle.

The rest of the night continued in a similar fashion, with us solving other puzzles and finding other kooky groups of people. At one point, we had to help find several different ingredients for the mad scientists to use in an experiment, as well as dramatically recite and act out lines from *Twilight*. It was absolutely hilarious and an incredible amount of fun. We weren't able to finish all of the puzzles by the end of the competition, but we still enjoyed every second.

CHAPTER THIRTY-FOUR

Roommate Experience

Living with five other girls takes some adjusting after only living with my parents and younger brother. Both Sara and I had never lived with roommates before, but our experience in Patterson 5207 was the perfect way to introduce us to the world of living independently and away from our family. Placing six girls from around the country in one apartment is an experience.

The six of us began our program hanging out all the time. We made sure everyone was included or at least invited to join us for any plans we made during our off days. I was impressed with how well we got along and fit together as roommates for the majority of our program. For simply finding a group of girls on Facebook from brief roommate surveys and short, casual conversations, I'd say I did a fairly good job with roommate hunting. We never had any huge drama, fights, or anything of the sort, which is somewhat of a miracle with that many girls sharing a small apartment for five months. The only problems we'd have were related to everyone doing their part when it came to cleaning the kitchen and preparing for inspection.

Inspection occurs once every couple months when Housing sends someone to inspect each apartment complex to make sure it was free of any prohibited items (weapons, drugs, the like), and ensure it was being kept clean (to Disney standards, which may be different than your standards). If you totally ace inspection with a beautifully clean and organized apartment, you and your roommates will receive the "White Glove Award", which includes a bin of delicious cookies. My roommates and I didn't try to win the White Glove Award during the first round of inspections, because we were pretty busy and only had time to clean just enough to pass.

When it came to our second round of inspections, we were motivated to receive that "White Glove Award". Many of us had the day off before inspection, so we dedicated most of our time to scrubbing the floors, polishing our kitchen, wiping down counters, vacuuming... you name it. If one of us had work, that person would still contribute to preparing and cleaning before or after their shift. However, one of my roommates was missing in action almost the entire day. I'm not going to mention any names, but no matter how often we tried to text her, call her, or message her on Facebook, we couldn't reach her. We knew she didn't have work that day, because we had a master schedule on a huge calendar in our living room printed with everyone's weekly shifts. By the time she finally returned to our apartment, we were nearly done cleaning. She informed us that she had been in the parks all day...needless to say, we weren't thrilled.

The cleanliness of the apartment was the main issue that caused conflict between the six of us. Apart from this, the inspection situation, and other minor personal disputes (in which I tried my best to remain uninvolved), we had some minor suspicions about someone possibly stealing food from the others without asking. Our suspicions could have been unfounded, and the thefts were so minor and infrequent that it never created a major issue.

What really got in the way of everyone remaining close were our work schedules. For example, Sarah's hours in Animal Kingdom were usually in the morning, while Carmen, Sara, Liz, and I normally worked at night in Magic Kingdom or at the resorts. Bethany worked in DisneyQuest and had mid-day or randomly scheduled shifts, which made it even more confusing to keep track. Naturally, if someone has a completely opposite work schedule than yours, you don't see them nearly as often as someone who has the same shifts. I grew close to Liz, not only because we had similar interests and our personalities clicked, but also because we had the similar night shifts, which meant she was able to drive me to work every once in a while.

Occasionally, there were special circumstances in which most (or sometimes all) of us would have the same days off. We'd take advantage of these opportunities to spend time together. I took my marketing class with Bethany, and so I was able to talk to her every Wednesday morning during our walks to and from our classroom in Chatham. Sometimes I would have a few consecutive morning shifts, which would allow me to hang out with Sarah.

As our program progressed, most of my roommates started to grow closer to their coworkers because they all had similar schedules, as well as spent nearly every day of the week together. I loved my coworkers, but I spent more time with people I met on Facebook and Tumblr before the program, such as Christine and Meriem.

The dynamic in our apartment began to shift when it came time to apply for program extensions. Carmen, Liz, and Sarah all applied to extend their programs and stay throughout the summer instead of leaving in May like Sara and me. Bethany applied to leave a week early, because summer classes at her college started before she was scheduled to go home. Carmen and Liz were accepted to extend their program, while Sarah went seasonal with Safaris (a position with Disney where you fulfill a certain number of hours per year, usually during the holiday seasons).

If you extend your program, you have to switch apartments if you don't have all of your roommates extending along with you. The original move-out date was June 1 for Liz and Carmen extending, but Carmen requested to move out earlier so she could move in with some friends she had made during her program. It was a little random, especially since she didn't tell us she was moving out nearly three weeks early. We found out through Bethany, who shared a room with Carmen. When the time came for her to move...she just left. There was no warning and she didn't say goodbye. We just came back from work one day and she was gone. She was still in Patterson, and Sara saw her at the bus stop every once in a while, but that was it.

I was able to hang with Bethany a little further into our program. I wish that our work schedules had allowed us to spend more time together. We explored DisneyQuest with Sara and Liz, which is definitely something to try if you're a fan of video games. We created virtual roller coasters, competed in a *Pirates of the Caribbean* simulator, and played every version of pinball offered on the top floor.

Overall, the important aspect of living with roommates is that you're all different people. You have varied work schedules and different personalities. It's possible to get along extremely well beforehand on Facebook, but then not stay friends once you start living together. The opposite could happen as well, where you barely communicate online and then grow very close during the program. Both of these instances happened to me, and I know other people who experienced similar situations. You just have to be prepared for anything!

CHAPTER THIRTY-FIVE

Graduation!

At the beginning of May, Disney hosts a fun little graduation party at Chatham Square for everyone who participated in the DCP. Sara, Bethany, and I went together and met up with Meriem and three of my friends from Capt. Cook's. When we arrived, we received our certificates of completion and graduation Mickey ears. The reception was filled with food, music, and an endless amount of pictures.

Disney characters dressed in graduation robes were scattered around the courtyard for pictures, including Goofy, Pluto, Donald, and Daisy. After we ate lunch, we waited in line to take pictures with Mickey and Minnie, who had their own special meet-and-greet area inside the Chatham classroom. While I was waiting in line I saw Jake and a few other friends, as well as the Disney ambassadors who casually strolled around to congratulate everyone on completing their program. Some of my friends from other countries were able to take pictures with flags from around the globe, including their national flag, which I found really neat.

It was Meriem's last day to explore the parks with us before her departure day, so after we took our pictures with Mickey and Minnie we went back to our apartment to change and then headed to Epcot. I took this opportunity to film another video, something I hadn't done in a while. Word of advice, if you plan on making videos or keeping a blog during your college program, make sure you dedicate the time and commit to keeping your YouTube channel or website up to date. It's easy to fall behind on posting or uploading videos, especially when you're working full time and playing in the parks on your days off. What usually happens is bloggers and vloggers are extremely active before their program and a little bit in the beginning, but once work hits full swing, many of them stop posting and uploading altogether. I didn't completely stop at any point. My posts and videos just became a little more sporadic than they were before my program.

In Epcot, we journeyed around Future World to ride Ellen's Energy Adventure for my first time and Mission: SPACE. We cruised through the World Showcase to visit Mexico and have dinner in Morocco before finding a seat for Illuminations, the beautiful nighttime fireworks show in Epcot (which Meriem had surprisingly never seen during her program). It was sad to know that this was many of the first "lasts" with certain friends near the end of our programs, but we knew it wasn't going to be the final time we saw each other. We ended the night with a quick trip to the BoardWalk to visit the newly renovated bakery, where Meriem and Sara got a cheesecake brownie while I devoured a peanut butter bar cake much quicker than I'd like to admit. It was a lovely evening, but unfortunately Meriem needed to head back to her apartment to finish packing before the big move back home the next day.

CHAPTER THIRTY-SIX

A Coronation, Star Wars, and the Christines

Some of my favorite memories from my internship occurred during the last month. For example, Meriem's official departure day coincided with Merida's official coronation in Magic Kingdom. After Meriem was all packed and ready to move out of her apartment, she brought her parents along with Liz, Sara, and me to witness the *Brave* princess' special day. We had no idea just how crowded the park was going to be for this celebration; the entire area in front of Cinderella Castle was already packed by the time we arrived a couple hours after the park opened.

We managed to find a spot to the right of Cinderella Castle up on the sidewalk with a decent view of the stage where the ceremony was going to be held. Right before the festivities began, the guest directly in front of us hoisted his child onto his shoulders, completely blocking our sight of the stage even though there was no one in front of him. We tried our best to maneuver around him to have any kind of view, but it still wasn't the best.

The ceremony began with two young girls from YouTube and *The Ellen Degeneres Show* named Sophia Grace and Rosie singing and rapping something, but the sound system was horrible and we couldn't understand a word they were saying. The situation improved once the actual coronation processes began. On stage, each of the current Disney princesses were introduced, as well as Olympic gold Mmedalist Gabby Douglas. Gabby and the hostess explained how each princess represents admirable qualities, such as Cinderella's kindness and graciousness.

Trumpets and bagpipes blared as a majestic Scottish band waltzed down Main Street toward the castle. Merida was following the band bareback on her massive black Scottish Clydesdale, Angus. She skipped her way up onto the stage and the hostess explained her admirable characteristics: "We do hereby declare, by virtue of her fiery spirit, independence, and her unwavering bravery, that Merida is officially welcome into the Disney princess royal court!"

The crowd cheered as Merida's mother, Queen Eleanor, emerged on stage to crown her daughter. I was glad I forced myself out of bed early to come and see this celebration. It certainly isn't something Disney guests or cast members get to see every day.

The end of the happy coronation also meant the beginning of something much more sad: it was time to say my first of many goodbyes. Meriem had to leave after the ceremony, and saying goodbye was something I really didn't want to face. We just turned around and looked at each other with sad expressions for a short moment, then grabbed each other for a hug right in front of the castle. I tried my best to conceal any tears, but it was difficult. She was one of the first friends I had made in the program, way back before we even knew whether we were accepted. We promised to keep in touch. Liz, Sara, and I had to try and focus on something else to distract us from how sad saying goodbye was going to be for the rest of the month, and that this was only the beginning.

We continued to make the most out of the last month of our program. Time was ticking and there wasn't a moment to waste. Sara, Liz, and I dedicated an entire day in Magic Kingdom to fulfill some final tasks on our bucket list: meet Merida (the last of all the princesses we needed to meet) and try a Nutella waffle and fruit sandwich at Sleepy Hollow, which was absolutely delicious. We also managed to ride the PeopleMover and see Space Mountain with the lights on.

Star Wars Weekends premiered in May. During this event, the *Star Wars* franchise takes over Hollywood Studios with character meet and greets, special shows, and limited edition merchandise, as well as meet and greets with actors from the movies and shows. I was usually working during these weekends, but one day I was able to attend with Sara and Marisa, a friend from Tumblr.

Our main goal was to meet all the rare characters. I wanted to meet Queen Amadala because her outfit is fantastic, but it started to rain while we were waiting in line and she had to return indoors for the rest of the day. However, we were able to meet Darth Maul and Darth Vader. Darth Maul was creepy...all he would do is stare at me with his blood-red eyes and snarl and snatch my autograph book out of my hand when given the chance. If you are a *Star Wars* fan, I recommend attending Star Wars Weekends. Some fans camp out in front of the Hollywood Studios entrance to guarantee priority entry and the ability to meet some of the actors from the series or purchase limited edition merchandise.

One of my all-time favorite memories from my program was "Christine Day". Liz, Sara, Christine, and I all had the same day off and decided to spend time in Animal Kingdom. There wasn't anything particularly different about this day, but the four of us could not stop smiling and laughing the entire time. There were hardly any lines, and we took one of my all-time favorite on-ride photos on DINOSAUR. We were the only guests in our Time Rover, so we all turned around and looked terrified as if the dinosaurs had eaten the rest of the guests. Later in the day, we were all enjoying lunch in Pizzafari and for some reason decided to mess with Facebook and change all of our profile pictures to the same photo of Christine. We kept commenting on each other's pictures, saying things like, "You look stunning!" followed by, "My, so do you!" From that moment, we called our little group Christine and the Christines.

Christine Day was our last day off in the parks together before the end of my program. Liz and Christine both were accepted to extend their program throughout the summer, but Sara and I only had a little over a week left. I couldn't believe just how quickly time was flying by.

CHAPTER THIRTY-SEVEN

Final Days at Capt. Cook's

The Spring 2013 college program Capt. Cook's crew started to dwindle after graduation. Carly, Nideria, and Megan all finished their programs a couple weeks before me. It was weird working in the restaurant without them, especially since the next DCP session and international cast members were starting to train and work with me. Every day I kept thinking about how my days at Cook's were numbered, and that pretty soon I'd be flying back to California.

Many of my other close friends were also beginning to leave. I joined Rebecca with some of her roommates on her last day in the parks at the last second, exploring every favorite ride in each park and ending the night with our favorite, the Electrical Parade, cheering on the Donkey Boys. I said goodbye to Megan, Carly, and Nideria when they visited work as guests for one last Dole Whip.

Whenever someone was close to finishing their program, we were always anxious to see what their final schedule was like. At midnight the week before my final shifts, I hovered over my laptop with anticipation, fingers crossed for a desirable schedule. I clicked refresh and looked at the calendar:

Every single shift ended at 1:30 in the morning.

I cackled. I had worked this shift so often that some of my coworkers had started calling me the designated 1:30 girl. It only seemed fitting that I was ending the program with my most commonly worked shift.

By the time I approached my final week at Capt. Cook's, I was mentally preparing myself for the late hours and overwhelming emotions. Part of me was excited to fly home. I missed my family, best friends, decent Mexican food, and even In-N-Out Burger (if you're from the West Coast, you'd understand). I couldn't wait to be able to drive myself to where I wanted to go without having to depend on unreliable transportation. However, the other part of me was absolutely devastated that I'd be leaving such an amazing life and incredible friends in Florida. I had made so many memories that all I wanted to do was continue to live my dream. I began to wonder where I would have been placed if I had extended my program and had requested a different location or role, but it was too late to dwell. My days as a Disney cast member were dwindling, and I needed to make the most out of every last moment.

My final few shifts at Cook's were similar. Since I had the 1:30 shift, I was mainly in charge of bussing the dining room and then helping the overnight cast member prepare for her long shift through the wee hours of the morning. The third shift cast member and I talked quite a bit during our cooperative preparation. It was interesting getting to know her, such as how she has been with the hotel since its first few opening years. I told her a lot about California and my family, and she could tell I was ready to go home. Five months was the longest I had ever been away from my family, so you could say I was growing a little homesick.

I was off early the night before my last shift, so I decided to see *Fantasmic!* with Sarah, Jake, and our other friend Andrea one last time. After the show, I said a final goodbye to Jake, which wasn't too emotional because he was planning on coming to visit me in California and Disneyland for the first time in the near future. Earlier in the day during my second to last shift, I said goodbye to coworker and friend Nick, which made me a little teary-eyed. Even though I was a little sad after saying goodbye to two close friends, I never even considered just how hard it would hit me after I finished my final shift at the Polynesian.

On May 28, I got dressed in the hideous shrub-patterned costume for the last time. Sara and I took pictures together in our costumes because we both were working our final shifts that night. I walked to the Chatham bus stop, arrived at the Poly, soaked in every beautiful detail of the gorgeous resort as I went backstage to clock in, and arrived at Capt. Cook's to see my last position in the restaurant: breaker.

I was thrilled.

I was worried I was going to be placed in the dining room for my last shift, which would have been rather anticlimactic and boring. I was grateful they had placed me on the breaker position, because it meant I was literally going to be working every position available one last time while I sent my coworkers on their breaks. This meant I'd be using both cash registers, cleaning the dining area, and most importantly, working behind the counter with my favorite culinary crew.

I was in charge of breaks from 6:00 to 8:45, and then it was my turn to go on break for around 15 minutes. When I returned from the break room, I helped a coworker behind the counter and then decided to walk out onto the beach to pick up trays around the pool. The best part about this idea was that I was able to watch a little bit of *Monsters Inc.,* since it was playing on a big screen on the beach that night. I brought the trays back to the dish room, threw out some food from the bakery that had spoiled, and then ran into my manager near the cooler.

She walked up to me and said, "Sara, how happy would you be if I gave you an ER on your last day?" (ER means early release from your shift.)

"You would be my most favorite person ever!" I squealed.

My manager opened her arms and pulled me in for a giant hug, "It's been an absolute pleasure working with you, and I wish you luck in all of your future goals back home."

My heart grew heavy. This was the first time she had ever said something along those lines to me. I was thankful for her kind words, but sad because my last shift spontaneously came to an end. I quickly walked into the kitchen to hug and say goodbye to one of the culinary cast members who had been a mother figure to me during my program. She was always so sweet and helpful whenever we worked together. I was going to miss working with her.

"Goodbye sweetheart, you've been a joy to have around and I'm going to miss having you behind the counter with us," she told me during our embrace.

I lost it. My eyes began to water and my ability to remain composed on stage in front of the guests was slipping. I snuck out the back and quickly walked around the patio to the cast member bathroom, covering my eyes with my hat so guests wouldn't notice I was crying. I locked myself in a bathroom stall and just let it all out. I couldn't stop crying no matter how hard I tried. It finally hit me that it was the last time I was going to work at Capt. Cook's. I only had one more full day in Walt Disney World. The hardest concept to grasp was that I wasn't going to be able to see my friends and co-workers every day.

I took a deep breath to compose myself after the tears started to die down. I splashed some water on my face from the sink and exited the bathroom to empty out my locker and clock out one final time. As I was walking through the parking lot to return my costumes across the street, I turned around and noticed the fireworks going off. I smiled and stood in the back of the parking lot for a little bit, simply to enjoy my last moments at the Poly. Just as the finale was starting, my favorite Iron Man monorail drove right under the fireworks and through the resort. The whole scenario was so perfect that I felt like I was in a movie.

I walked across the street to Costuming and bid goodbye to the orange pants and tacky floral. No more resembling a piece of furniture every day! For the entire bus ride home I kept brainstorming about how I was going to finish packing my life away into only two suitcases and one backpack, and what Sara and I were going to do to spend our last day here. It suddenly hit me:

Four parks. One day.

Challenge accepted.

CHAPTER THIRTY-EIGHT

"See Ya Real Soon!"

Sara and I woke up bright and early to meet Christine for our quest to do the unthinkable: visit all four Walt Disney World parks in one day. Some of our friends had attempted this challenge during our program, but we never had the energy to go to more than two during an average day. Our strategy was to first visit Animal Kingdom, then Epcot, have Liz join us at Hollywood Studios, and end our night in Magic Kingdom.

Animal Kingdom was rather quick, since we just wanted to conquer Everest and DINOSAUR one last time, as well as take a photo in front of the Tree of Life. We didn't have any specific plans for Epcot, so first we made our way to Club Cool to try different flavored sodas from around the world (even force down a "shot" of Beverly...the most bitter drink I've ever experienced). Since it was the end of May and summer break was beginning for many guests, the parks were growing more crowded than usual. Due to the increased volume, we weren't able to ride any attractions except for Spaceship Earth, which usually has waits not much longer than ten minutes.

Liz texted me that she was up and ready to meet us at Hollywood Studios, so the three of us quickly took pictures in front of Spaceship Earth and drove to visit my favorite park one last time. I was disheartened to see how busy Hollywood Studios was when we arrived in the early afternoon. We first took pictures in front of the Sorcerer Hat and nearly sprinted down Sunset Boulevard to see the wait times for Tower of Terror and Rock 'n' Roller Coaster. Sadly, both were over 45 minutes to an hour, and the single rider line was closed for Coaster (which usually significantly cuts wait time if you're okay riding on your own). We decided on Tower for our final ride in Studios, since I love the ride so much and the wait was a little bit shorter.

The wait was miserable. Christine, Sara, and I (Liz doesn't like Tower) were stuck behind a loud and obnoxious group of 15 year olds from Brazil. They kept running in and out of line, chanting and singing at the top of their lungs, and clapping and shrieking at any opportune moment. I'd send annoyed glares their direction whenever they were being loud, which they noticed. I could tell they were talking about me at one point (even though I can't understand Portuguese), but I didn't care. Everyone should be courteous of other guests waiting in line, especially if you're standing next to each other for nearly an hour. I was thankful that they weren't placed on the same elevator as us, so I was still able to enjoy every moment of my favorite attraction.

It was time to head to Magic Kingdom. We first visited Liz in Le Chapeau on Main Street so she could engrave our names and "DCP Spring 2013" on the back of our special graduation ears before tackling any final rides. Most of the night in Magic Kingdom was spent visiting friends, taking pictures, and reminiscing about everything we loved about our program. These past five months absolutely flew by; I couldn't believe I was about to watch Celebrate the Magic, Wishes, and the Main Street Electrical Parade for one final time as a DCP cast member.

When the three of us found a perfect spot to watch these shows for the last time, I could already feel myself grow emotional about the end of my program. The lights dimmed for Celebrate the Magic and my throat tightened. Through every scene that transformed Cinderella Castle through Disney movie history, I recalled moments during my program. From the very first time I saw the show, to watching it more than once in a night with some of my best friends, to experiencing my family's first time watching both night shows, these were all memories I would never forget.

However, once the *Lilo and Stitch* scene started dancing on the castle, my heart stopped. I immediately flashed back to my final night in the Polynesian, and all of the guests and friends I had made in such a beautiful resort. I remembered "Aloha Day", at the end of my Polynesian orientation, when all new cast members were required to dance the hula in front of everyone in the hotel lobby. I remembered how guests both young and old would light up with excitement in their eyes whenever I asked about their vacations. I remembered singing and quoting *Pitch Perfect* with my coworkers while filling out orders behind the counter. Food and Beverage may have not been my original first choice, but I would not change my role or experience for the world.

Watching Wishes that night was an emotional experience. I remembered the first time I had watched the show at the beginning of my program, and in that moment truly realizing that my dreams were coming true. I couldn't believe that I had officially finished my internship, something I had only dreamt about exactly a year ago. I really did it. I prepared, applied, got accepted, and moved to the other side of the country to work for Disney. I never expected to create such close and meaningful friendships with fellow cast members. Even though I only knew some of these wonderful people for only five months (sometimes less), I felt like I had known them for a lifetime. I couldn't even imagine what it was going to be like moving back home the next day, not knowing when I would ever see them again.

I managed to fight back tears during the Wishes finale, and then grabbed Christine and Sara for a hug. We were surrounded by other college program cast members with their special graduation ears hugging their friends and crying about the end of their programs. Our last moments in the park were spent taking photos in front of the castle and walking down a nearly empty Main Street as the park was about to close. It was finally time to head back to my apartment and return to reality, where a suitcase was waiting for me to fill it with all of my belongings and stow it on a plane bound for California.

We had visitors come to our apartment to say goodbye as Sara and I were attempting to finish packing for our flight home. It was crazy knowing that those moments were possibly the last time I was going to see some of them, especially since a few of my friends were from other countries. I'll always remember hugging my sweet Brazilian coworker Rodolpho in front of the security gate to Patterson (since he lived in Vista Way), just crying in each other's arms while we said goodbye. I told everyone that if they ever ended up traveling to Disneyland to tell me so I could see them again. Everyone in the DCP had a saying that we weren't actually saying goodbye. Each goodbye really meant, "See ya real soon!" We knew this wasn't the last time we were going to see each other. We knew that someday down the line, we would cross paths once again. Many of our friendships were too strong and special to give up simply because we were going home.

By midnight, we were done packing. We knew we needed to go to sleep, but we weren't tired. Christine, Liz, Sara, and I spend most of the night together in my apartment, just talking and complaining about how we weren't ready to go home. Finally, the four of us embraced in one last group hug and said goodbye to Christine. Sara and I ended up hanging out with Mitch and talking until nearly six in the morning. Let's just say the sun was coming up and cast members were heading to Animal Kingdom for work already.

And just like that, my Disney College Program was over.

CHAPTER THIRTY-NINE

Returning Home

Liz and Sarah drove Sara and me to the airport so we could catch our long flight home. We were nearly dragging our feet to the plane because we were so fatigued from the adventures of park hopping the day before. Saying goodbye to Liz and Sarah was tough, but I focused on the positives and how I was going to see my parents and brother for the first time since they visited nearly two months ago, and see my best friend Holly for the first time in over five months.

With our rotten luck, a storm in New Orleans delayed our flight from departing on time, causing us to miss our connector flight in Colorado and requiring Sara and me to wait nearly three hours instead of the scheduled 45 minutes during our layover in the dull Denver airport.

When we finally made it home, I was overjoyed to see both of our moms waiting for us at the end of the terminal. My mom snatched me into the biggest hug and then surprised us with the news that we would be going to In-N-Out Burger during the ride back home for our first meal back in California.

This was the best news I had heard since leaving Florida.

The drive home consisted mainly of stories about how our families had been doing while we were away, the latest gossip about our small town community, and of course our never-ending stories about our latest adventures during the last few weeks of our programs.

It was strange dropping Sara and her mom off at her house, and even stranger pulling into my family's driveway. I had never been away from home for so many consecutive months; my house even smelled a little differently than I remembered (I could smell our dogs a little more strongly than I could before). I walked into my room and noticed that everything was in its place exactly how I had left it five months ago.

I sat down on my bed and cried.

All of my friends were on the other side of the country.

I couldn't wake up next week and feel like traveling to Hollywood Studios.

I would no longer go to work every day to make magic for guests. Now what?

CHAPTER FORTY

Post DCP Depression

I tried my best to distract myself from the fact that I was back in reality and not living in the Disney bubble. However, no matter how hard I tried, I would always find myself either looking at old photos from my program, watching Disney movies, listening to music from the parks, singing Disney songs wherever I went...the list goes on. Thankfully, I wasn't the only person going through this experience after moving back home. The only thing Sara and I could seem to talk about was our program and how much we missed everyone.

Past program participants would say that my actions were symptoms of something we call Post DCP Depression. Let me just say that this is a real disease, and it's rather sad. Adjusting to life back home was much more difficult than I thought. After a few weeks of focusing on how I wasn't in the college program anymore, I started to shift my way of thinking. In only a couple months, I was going to move to a new city once again. I needed to make the most out of being home, as well as prepare for transferring schools. I had enough to keep me busy during the summer, such as registering for classes, orientation, deciding what to bring for my new apartment, and discovering who I was going to live with for the next year. On top of all this, there was something I knew I needed to do as soon as possible.

I needed a job in Disneyland.

Every day, first thing in the morning, I would check online to see if Disneyland had any openings for part-time cast members. I was especially looking for attractions or merchandise positions, but I had an open mind for any role. There was an opening in early July for a position as a PhotoPass Photographer, but there was no way I could make it to southern California (a nine-hour drive) at the last minute to attend an in-person interview. I needed to wait and apply around when I was going to move...which required me to remain patient for at least another month.

I started to discover a difference about myself since I returned home from Disney World. Aside from constantly singing Disney songs around the house and shamelessly watching shows from the Disney parks on YouTube, I had a much higher level of self-confidence. Before my program, I was rather shy. While working as a front desk receptionist for my dad's chiropractic office, I was always somewhat hesitant about speaking to new people, answering the phone, or calling insurance companies. The couple times I worked in the office after the college program, I noticed that I was much more confident and comfortable with greeting patients when they arrived and never thought twice about calling people on the phone (dealing with insurance companies was still not my favorite task, but it was a little less intimidating compared to how it had been before my program).

It was tough not having a Mickey sticker to give to a crying child or calling a little girl "princess" out in public. I never failed to point with two fingers (called the "Disney Point") and always knelt down whenever I talked to children. In all honesty, I was a little awkward talking to kids before I worked for Disney. Nowadays, you can't get me to stop!

Above all, my goal each day was to keep the Disney spirit alive each day. Whether it was remaining patient with a struggling cashier (I had a newfound empathy for food service workers) or helping other people with anything they might need, I tried my best to emulate positivity and to bring kindness into the lives of others. Even though I was no longer working in a Disney resort, that didn't stop me from making at least a little magic in small ways for other people each day.

CHAPTER FORTY-ONE

New Opportunities

The big day to move to my new school was slowly creeping up on me. Pretty soon, I only had a week left at home. Even though I was about to make such a huge change and move to a new city, I only had one fact on my mind: I could now apply for work at Disneyland. I heard on Tumblr that it took at least a week to schedule an interview after you send in your initial application. Some people wouldn't even hear back for months after they applied.

I woke up each morning with hope in my heart and routinely checked the Disney Careers website for any potential openings. Every day had the same result: nothing. I would bounce back and forth in my head on whether I would prefer working in merchandise or attractions, but I knew that if any of these roles popped up online I wouldn't think twice about applying.

One Friday morning I woke up and went through the same routine: open laptop, check website, sigh, and then spend most of the day preparing for moving. Around mid-afternoon, I took a break from packing and Skyped with Jake. We started reminiscing our programs and I discussed my plans for moving the following week while he was making pizza.

"I just want a job to open in Disneyland already. I'm growing impatient," I sighed.

"When was the last time you checked?" Jake questioned.

"I check literally every single morning! Sometimes I look multiple times later in the day!" I threw my hands up in the air.

He shrugged, "Just have to wait, I guess."

"Look, I'll even check again and nothing will be there..."

I went to my bookmarks and clicked on the Disney Careers site, still complaining about how nothing's probably changed since that morning.

I froze.

At the top of the list of job postings was attractions.

"OH MY GOD!!!" I screamed and nearly fell out of my chair.

"WHAT?!" Poor Jake had no idea what had just happened.

"ATTRACTIONS IS OPEN FOR PART TIME! OH MY GOSH!!"

I clicked on the link to the application and snatched my phone to update all my friends. My mom coincidentally arrived home from the grocery store a few seconds after I discovered the job opening and told me to get off Skype and apply immediately. I apologized to Jake and logged off to focus on my application. The application was very similar to the one I filled out for the DCP, except this one didn't have a section to rank your interest in roles (since it was specific for attractions). An hour after I finished the application, I was invited to take the web-based interview, which was exactly the same as the one I did for the college program. Immediately after I finished the WBI, I was invited to schedule my final step: an in-person interview.

I threw my hands up in the air and squealed as I ran out into the living room to tell my mom that I got an interview. We scheduled it for exactly a week later, only a few days after I moved in to my new apartment. Now I was not only excited and nervous about moving to a new city and meeting new people, but I might have a job in the role I've always wanted.

Next Friday couldn't arrive fast enough.

CHAPTER FORTY-TWO

A New Chapter

Next week, I packed all of my belongings into the trunk of my car and said goodbye to my dad, brother, and pets before hopping behind the steering wheel with my mom and heading off on my new adventure, nine hours away. I had always flown to southern California, not driven. After experiencing the tedious and never-ending journey, I decided to stick to flying the next time I visited home.

We stayed in a hotel the night before move-in day on campus, and all I could think about was my interview. Unlike the phone interview for the DCP, I couldn't find too many sample questions online from previous part-time interviews for Disneyland attractions. I did discover that many people who went into their interviews for a specific role came out hired in a different department. For example, someone could be invited for an interview in merchandise, but get offered a position in hotel front desk if it's the only role available at the time. I was a little worried that they would ask me to take a position in foods again, since they were hiring for that department as well, but I just had to wait and see.

The next day I moved into my new place and met all five of my roommates. Some of them were big Disney fans, and I had already met another person who worked at Disneyland on my floor. I took my mom to the airport, gave her a hug goodbye, and finished unpacking for the rest of the night. I had a few errands to run before Friday, which helped keep my mind off of my interview for a little bit. I wasn't necessarily nervous, but more anxious to know whether I was going to join the Disney family again.

Finally, Friday morning arrived. I drove to Disneyland's casting center, checked in with the front desk, and waited with a group of other hopeful cast members. Butterflies were starting to flutter in my stomach as I tried to mentally practice a few of the practice questions I had found online. A few minutes later, a recruiter opened the door.

"Sara?"

My fellow hopefuls wished me luck as I took a deep breath and entered the room. The recruiter greeted me and shook my hand before I sat down on the other side of her desk. I had my answer to the typical opening question ("Why do you want to work for Disney?") prepared and on the tip of my tongue as my recruiter initiated the interview.

"So it says you've worked for the company before. Why do you want to come back?"

I froze. This question was too easy.

"I want a career with the company."

"Okay, great."

I didn't even need to explain myself; the answer seemed to work just fine with her. She continued with a few more basic questions such as details about my work history (specifically for more information about my college program) and my preferences for working conditions. She also asked a few more attractions-related questions such as, "If a child wasn't tall enough to ride your attraction, what would you do?"

"I'd apologize to the family, explain that it's for their safety, and then show them other attractions they all can enjoy together."

My recruiter nodded and smiled, "Well, Sara, welcome to Disneyland Attractions."

I nearly squealed while she continued, "We only have openings in California Adventure; is that okay?"

I grinned, "Well, I've always wanted to work Tower of Terror...so that's perfect!"

"Alright! I'll place you in Hollywood Land."

Just like that, I was a cast member again.

I returned a week later to fill out more paperwork and then attended Traditions around a month later. My Traditions class for Disneyland was more or less the same as the one I went through in Walt Disney World, just with a smaller class size. My second day of orientation was called My California Story, which was required for all cast members who were going to work in California Adventure. This was one of my favorite orientations, because we were able to take a tour of the entire park and learn about every single detail of history and meaning behind each area of the resort, its attractions, and its restaurants. Every time we learned something new during the tour, we had to shout "Eureka!" (A cute way to stick to the California theme.) This was my first time experiencing California Adventure since they redesigned the park to add Buena Vista Street and Cars Land. I loved learning about the connection between Buena Vista Street and Walt's early career in Hollywood, as well as walking down Route 66 for the very first time.

My final day of general Disneyland orientation was Welcome to Park Operations. This class was specifically designed for incoming cast members involved with roles that served as key positions for operating the park. Custodial, guest relations, and attractions are a few of the many roles we discussed and explored throughout the day. I was particularly excited about this orientation for one particular reason: this was the day I'd learn my location.

At the end of Welcome to Park Operations, I chatted excitedly with some new friends while our instructors distributed everyone's information packets with our training schedules and locations. All of us were anxiously wondering about which attraction we were going to work. Everyone already knew which section they were going to be in, such as Fantasyland, Toontown, or (like myself) Hollywood Land.

I held my breath as a woman handed me my info pamphlet. I looked at the bold red letters on the front to see where I was placed: Disney Animation.

I wasn't quite sure what to think, because I hadn't even been inside the Animation building since I was in middle school. All I remembered is that there was Turtle Talk With Crush, which was really neat. (Guests could actually talk to Crush from *Finding Nemo*.) Nonetheless, I was excited to start working. What mattered the most is that I was a cast member again, already making new friends and giddy with anticipation to make new magic.

CHAPTER FORTY-THREE

Back to the Beginning

Before my training began, I was called up to meet with the man in charge of new-hire scheduling. Unfortunately, Animation was going under refurbishment during my scheduled training days. The scheduler gave me the option to either transfer to Paradise Pier to keep my original days of training, or to stay in Hollywood and postpone training to the following weekend. Without any hesitation I told him I wanted to stay in Hollywood, so he told me I'd get a call in the following week about my new location.

True to his word, I got the call a week later to come in the next day for my first in-park training shift, called Guest Interaction Training (GIT). Along with my trainer and another girl who was training with me, we went to Costuming to change into our guest control costumes and my training buddy's costume for Soarin' Over California. The guest control costume was a snazzy looking red vest, bowtie, white pants, and slightly poufy-sleeved blouse. It was definitely a step up from my last costume, with its tacky Hawaiian printed glory.

Most of the day consisted of walking around every inch of California Adventure. Our trainer showed us where all the bathrooms, ATM machines, smoking sections, and churro carts were located. The main goal of Guest Interaction Training was to give us a basic understanding of the park to make sure we could answer frequently asked questions from guests when we started working at our attractions and guest control shifts.

"In the beginning of your time working here, you'll mainly see guest control shifts instead of your attraction. You'll mainly work the Pixar Play Parade and World of Color."

A smile immediately sprouted on my face when my trainer mentioned World of Color. The thought of getting paid to work and possibly watch the show that inspired me to work for Disney was unreal. I kept this thought in the back of my head for the rest of training, which consisted mostly of answering guest questions and learning how to set up ropes and poles for the parade. Toward the end of our shift, we observed cast members setting up and organizing the viewing area for World of Color.

As we approached show time, our trainer turned to us and grinned, "So, do you want to watch the show?"

I'm pretty sure the noise I made in response wasn't human, but I was internally bouncing off the walls. I hadn't seen World of Color since my first experience two years ago, and to watch it again as a cast member is something my 18-year-old self would never believe.

We walked up to the empty queue for the Little Mermaid attraction to view the show away from the guests. My stomach fluttered with anticipation as the lights dimmed and the majestic music began to play.

"The world is a carousel of color..."

As water and color danced along the bay, I started to reminisce back to the first time I watched the show. Something clicked. This was the show that inspired me to want to become a cast member and work for Disney. Because of this show, I went home to search jobs and discovered the Disney College Program. Because of this show, I took a risk, followed my dream, and had an incredibly memorable experience that completely changed my life.

Now I'm here, I thought to myself. *Now I'm working the show that started it all.*

It's incredible to think that my spark of inspiration from watching World of Color brought me to such an amazing experience as the Disney College Program. Even though I always knew that it would be an unforgettable, I never expected to meet and create lifelong friendships with people who shared my interests and dreams.

Whenever someone tells me that they're considering applying to the DCP, I tell them to go for it. The experience of traveling to a new place, meeting new people, growing as an individual both personally and professionally, and having a chance to meet and make magic for guests around the globe is something you will remember and cherish forever. From the guest who would call me Snow White every day at the Polynesian, to the various adorable pirates and princesses I would give stickers to whenever possible, I will hold every interaction close to my heart.

Applying for The Disney College Program was the first step in a journey filled with incredible friends and memorable experiences. Even though I didn't get the role I originally wanted during my program, working at Capt. Cook's introduced me to wonderful coworkers and memories that will last me a lifetime. When I officially "earned my ears", I accomplished a goal that I would have found nearly impossible only one year ago.

To have the ability to wake up every day and remind myself that I was living the life I had only dreamed about in the past is something I will truly never, ever forget.

College Program Helpers

Phone Interview Study Guide

Here is a list of questions I used to prepare for the ever-daunting Disney College Program phone interview. I've included general questions—the kind they're likely to ask everyone—and specific questions by role. Make sure you're familiar with the questions associated with the role(s) you selected on your application.

General Questions

- Why do you want to work with Disney?
- Why do you want to participate in the program?
- What does it mean to you to be a Disney cast member?
- What makes you a good candidate for the DCP?
- What can you offer the company?
- What does Disney mean to you?
- Have you been to Disney World? What did you like about it? What's your favorite memory there, and why? Describe a magic moment you've had in the Disney parks.
- Are you familiar with the Disney parks and other parks in the area?
- What does being in Florida mean to you?
- Do you think it would be a big adjustment to move this far from home?
- Share an experience you've had with excellent guest service.
- What do you want to get out of this internship?
- Why did you choose to apply to this internship at this moment in your college career?
- How do you think the program will help you professionally?

- Rank your top three roles. Why?
- Would you be open to working _____ role?
- At which park or resort would you prefer to work? (Tip: Take a look at the location's hours, attractions, restaurants, shops, etc. before you make your selection.)
- What would you do if your apartment roommates weren't cleaning up after themselves?
- How do you feel about living with 1–7 roommates?
- What part of the housing situation are you most looking forward to?
- What would you do if a roommate wouldn't cooperate with your sleep schedule?
- Previous work experience?
- If you've had a job before, what did you like and dislike about it?
- Talk about an experience you've had with good customer service.
- In what ways would you provide excellent guest service?
- Name three positive qualities about yourself.
- What are some words your employer, coworker, or professor would use to describe you?
- Describe a situation where you had to work with a difficult person. (Boss, coworker, professor, customer, etc.)
- How would you handle an emergency at the parks?
- What are you most looking forward to in the program?
- Have you ever handled money?
- How would you greet guests?
- How would you manage getting tasks completed while being interrupted by guests, etc.?
- How would you feel about working outdoors?
- Do you prefer to work as a team or individually?
- At what pace do you prefer to work?
- How would you handle a guest who needs help but doesn't speak your language?
- Describe a time at your job when you made someone happy.

Attractions

- Have you ever had to give a presentation for a lot of people, using a microphone? How did you feel doing so?
- What would you do if you were working an attraction and a guest was too short to ride?
- Have you ever had to memorize a presentation and then deliver it in front of a group of people?
- What experience have you had speaking in front of crowds? Are you comfortable doing so?
- What would you do if you messed up your spiel?
- If you were doing a task that was repetitive (spieling, etc.), how would you keep yourself interested in it?
- How would you feel if you were interrupted doing a task?

PhotoPass Photographer

- What experience do you have working with cameras?

Main Gate/Transportation

- How would you maintain the magic in Main Gate operations?
- Why do you think transportation is so important at Disney?

Hotel/Concierge

- What would you do if you were working the front desk and a guest wanted a specific type of room but none were available?
- How comfortable would you be being trained on and working with a computer reservation system?
- How would you make a guest feel special if they are just starting their Disney vacation?
- What do you think the duties of a concierge are?
- How are you experienced for this role?

Bibbidi Bobbidi Boutique

- What would you do if you were working at the Bibbidi Bobbidi Boutique and had a timid princess who wasn't very receptive to getting her hair and makeup done?

Character Attendant

- Why do you want to be a character attendant?
- How is [certain character] in two parks at once?
- Why can't characters talk?
- What would you do if a child was rough with the character?
- What does character integrity mean to you?
- What would you do if a child was afraid of a character?
- What would you tell guests if you had to turn them away because a line was closed for the day?

Merchandise

- What would you do if you were working merchandise and the store didn't have the specific Tinker Bell shirt a girl was looking for?
- What would you do if a guest wanted a specific item that you did not carry anywhere in your park?
- You will have to be able to pin trade with customers. Will you be comfortable with children touching your lanyard and asking to trade?
- Your phone starts to ring while you're helping a guest in front of you. What do you do?

Custodial

- Have you ever had experience cleaning?
- Can you handle talking to multiple people and multi-tasking?
- Are you allergic to any chemicals, cleaning supplies, or latex?
- Can you handle working outside for up to eight hours a day?

Packing List

This is the basic list I used to pack for the big move to Florida. I took a plane, so if you're driving you might be able to bring more on your journey and buy less after you arrive.

Clothes

- Jeans
- Shorts
- Yoga pants
- Three sweatshirts
- Raincoat
- Two Pajama pants & shirts
- Pajama shorts
- Workout shorts/spandex
- LOTS of underwear
- LOTS of socks (white/black)
- Long-sleeved shirts
- T-Shirts
- Workout shirts
- Tank tops
- Bathing Suits
- Nice pants
- Professional shirts
- Everyday shoes
- Workout Shoes
- Flats
- Sandals
- Boots
- Bathrobe/towel thing
- Jacket

Other

- Passport, license, Social Security card/important forms

- Alarm clock
- Computer and case
- Phone and charger
- Camera
- Pillow/Pillow Pet
- Toothbrush/toothpaste
- Brush/comb
- Earrings
- Makeup
- Face wash
- Hat/sunglasses
- Movies/games
- Straightener/hair dryer
- Hair ties/bobby pins
- Deodorant
- Router
- Backpack
- Books
- Journal
- Pens/pencils

Buy in Florida

- Hangers
- Shampoo/conditioner
- Body wash
- Razors
- Bedding
- Mattress pad
- Bath towels
- Hand towels
- Pool towel
- Shower curtain/curtain rings

- Laundry basket
- Lamp
- Lock for lockers
- Bath rug
- Soap
- Toilet paper
- Surge protecter

DCP Roommate Survey

This is the roommate survey I used when trying to find people to live with during my program. I posted the completed survey on the Spring 2013 DCP Facebook page and waited to see if anyone was interested in getting to know Sara and me as potential roommates. Not only did I use this survey to find roommates, it was also a helpful tool to meet people with similar interests, some of whom became great friends.

Background

- Name:
- Gender:
- Orientation:
- Relationship status:
- Birthday/age:
- Location:
- From:
- School:
- Major:
- Allergies:
- Siblings:

DCP Details

- Are you applying for WDW or DL?
- Flying or driving:
- Your role?:
- What program are you applying for?

- Do you want to live in Wellness or Non-Wellness?
- How many people do you want to live with?
- Which housing complex would you like to live in?:
- Alumni?

Lifestyle

- Do you party? How often?
- Do you smoke?
- Do you drink?
- Can you cook?
- Are you a night person or a morning person?
- Do you snore?
- What does your bedroom normally look like?
- Do you like it when your room is hot or cold?
- Would you rather go out or stay in?
- What do you like to do on your days off/the weekend?
- Do you work out a lot?

Personality

- Three words that describe you:
- One good quality:
- One bad quality:
- Are you outgoing or quiet?
- Do you like hanging out with people or keeping to yourself?
- What would you want in a roommate?
- What are your biggest pet peeves/dislikes?
- Are you messy or organized?
- How do you feel about sharing?
- Do you like having people over a lot?
- Favorite thing to do:
- Favorite music:
- Favorite TV shows:
- Favorite movies:

- Favorite food:
- Favorite candy:
- Favorite drink:
- Favorite color:

Disney

- Favorite character:
- Favorite movie:
- Favorite Disney Channel show:
- Favorite park:
- Favorite ride:

Websites

The Disney Den
http://www.thedisneyden.com

This is the blog I created before my college program. Here you can find news and updates about all things Disney, as well as advice, information, and interviews of past alumni from the DCP.

Official Disney College Program Site
http://cp.disneycareers.com

Everything you need to know about the Disney College Program, including living situations, classes, role descriptions, and much more.

About the Author

Sara Lopes is a born-and-raised Disney fan who's had the opportunity to work at both the Walt Disney World Resort in Florida as well as at Disneyland in California. She will graduate from California State University, Fullerton, in Fall 2015 with a degree in marketing.

Sara is an avid blogger and Netflix addict, and runs the popular website The Disney Den [TheDisneyDen.com].

About the Publisher

Theme Park Press is the largest independent publisher of Disney and Disney-related pop culture books in the world.

Established in November 2012 by Bob McLain, Theme Park Press has released best-selling print and digital books about such topics as Disney films and animation, the Disney theme parks, Disney historical and cultural studies, park touring guides, autobiographies, fiction, and more.

For more information, and a list of forthcoming titles, please visit:

ThemeParkPress.com

More Books from Theme Park Press

Amber Earns Her Ears

My Boss, Mickey Mouse

Come read Amber Sewell's Disney College Program diary and share her successes and her failures, her moments of delight and her moments of despair, and learn what happens when the pixie dust settles and the guests have gone home.

Earning Your Ears: Volume 1

ThemeParkPress.com/books/amber-earns-her-ears.htm

Ema Earns Her Ears

God Save the Mouse

Ema Hutton's two summers in Disney's International College Program took her from a little town in England to cleaning rooms at Port Orleans and performing as Pluto in the Magic Kingdom. Ema gives the most revealing glimpse yet of working backstage at Disney World.

Earning Your Ears: Volume 2

ThemeParkPress.com/books/ema-earns-her-ears.htm

More Books from Theme Park Press

The Ride Delegate

Disney World for the 1%

The rich and famous experience Disney World differently from the rest of us: they're escorted by VIP Tour Guides, elite Cast Members who truly do hold the keys to the kingdom. Come meet the eccentric, outrageous guests who turned former VIP Tour Guide Annie Salisbury's life into a reality show.

ThemeParkPress.com/books/ride-delegate.htm

The Unauthorized Story of Walt Disney's Haunted Mansion

Welcome, Foolish Readers!

Haunted Mansion expert Jeff Baham recounts the colorful, chilling history of the Mansion and pulls back the shroud on its darkest secrets in this definitive book about Disney's most ghoulish attraction.

Foreword by Rolly Crump.

ThemeParkPress.com/books/haunted-mansion.htm

More Books from Theme Park Press

Murder in the Magic Kingdom

Who's Killing Walt Disney World Cast Members?

A body has turned up in the waters of the Jungle Cruise and Disney wants to pin the murder on Cast Member Josh Bates. With security closing in, Josh must race through the theme parks to solve the murderer's maddening riddles and clear his name.

ThemeParkPress.com/ books/murder-magic.htm

Two Girls and a Mouse Tale

Double Shot of the Disney College Program!

Two girls from Colorado spend a year in the College Program at Walt Disney World, balancing pixie dust with reality bites, as they spin magic for guests in the parks, but can't talk their roommates into keeping the apartment clean.

ThemeParkPress.com/books/ two-girls-mouse-tale.htm

Discover our many other popular titles at:

www.ThemeParkPress.com

Made in the USA
Columbia, SC
28 September 2017